THAT
NONE SHOULD PERISH
ETHIOPIA 1933–1937

THE FIVE-YEAR DIARY OF MABEL STREET

Harold B. Street, Jr.

That None Should Perish, Ethiopia 1933-1937
The Five-Year Diary of Mabel Street
All Rights Reserved.
Copyright © 2019 Harold B. Street, Jr.
v1.0

The opinions expressed in this manuscript are solely the opinions of the author and do not represent the opinions or thoughts of the publisher. The author has represented and warranted full ownership and/or legal right to publish all the materials in this book.

This book may not be reproduced, transmitted, or stored in whole or in part by any means, including graphic, electronic, or mechanical without the express written consent of the publisher except in the case of brief quotations embodied in critical articles and reviews.

Outskirts Press, Inc.
http://www.outskirtspress.com

ISBN: 978-1-9772-0783-8

Cover Photo © 2019 Audrey Scott, UncorneredMarket.com. All Rights Reserved – Used With Permission.

Cover and interior design © 2019 Otto Dimitrijevics. All Rights Reserved – Used With Permission.

Quoted Scriptures are from the King James Version in the Public Domain.

Scriptures marked "NASB" are taken from the NEW AMERICAN STANDARD BIBLE®, Copyright (c) 1960, 1962, 1963, 1968, 1971, 1972, 1973, 1975, 1977, 1995 by The Lockman Foundation. Used by permission.

Map of Ethiopia was prepared by the Sudan Interior Mission and used with their permission.

Excerpt from "Much More Than Survival" was written by C. P. Hia, Our Daily Bread®, copyright © 2014 by Our Daily Bread Ministries, Grand Rapids, MI. Reprinted by permission. All rights reserved.

Outskirts Press and the "OP" logo are trademarks belonging to Outskirts Press, Inc.

PRINTED IN THE UNITED STATES OF AMERICA

outskirts press

*In honor of Mabel and Harold Street
and the many other faithful servants of the Lord,
this book is dedicated to the glory of God
and His great love for us.*

"Missions represents not a human devise,
but a Divine enterprise."

A. T. Pierson

Table of Contents

Acknowledgements ix
Introduction 1

Chapter 1
    Following the Call 3

Chapter 2
    1933, Addis Ababa and Furi, Ethiopia 13

Chapter 3
    1934, Furi and Soddo 33

Chapter 4
    1935, Soddo and Gamo 65

Chapter 5
    1936, Gamo, Soddo, and War 85

Chapter 6
    1937, Soddo, Addis Ababa, and the Return 115

Chapter 7
    All Things for the Gospel's Sake 131

Chapter 8
    The Mission Continues 133

Chapter 9
    Reflecting on God's Blessings 141

Chapter 10
    Childhood Memories of Hal and Paul 143

Chapter 11
- *Surprise! Small World* 147

Appendix A
- *People and Places in the Diary* 151

Appendix B
- *Quotes from Mabel's New Testament* 157

Acknowledgements

To Harold and Mabel Street for leading exemplary lives of love and service for their God to thousands of those in need in Ethiopia and around the world. To Mabel for her daily diary entries as well as notes she had written on the back of various pictures from Ethiopia and the United States.

To Janice Street for her contributions and pictures from the Street Genealogy.

To Laurie Reek for all of her help to transform handwritten copies into computer form. This was a true labor of love.

To Mary-Reid Warner for her help editing and proofreading to more adequately relate the power of God in the family of Mabel and Harold Street.

To Fran Taylor for her editorial contributions, suggestions, and general guidance to assist in the progress of the book.

To Tim Geysbeek of SIM International for providing the map of 1930s Ethiopia and a very helpful article on the history of SIM in Ethiopia.

To Michael DeLon and Ottó Dimitrijevics for their publishing expertise, recommendations, and for preparing the story for print and publication.

To my Lord who enabled me to have the opportunity to share this true love story of His grace and power as a challenge for others to emulate.

To God be the glory!

Introduction

Most of us enjoy hearing or reading a good story, especially if the story is true and propels us into the unknown. This is such a narrative. The primary source of this account is the Five-Year Diary with entries made daily by Mabel Street, a missionary in Ethiopia, Africa. The diary covers the years from 1933 to 1937.

At this time Ethiopia, with its rugged mountains and largely undeveloped areas, was beset by tribal wars. It had not been invaded by outside powers until Mussolini and the Italian armies conquered the country in 1936–37. Many European countries enhanced their world power by establishing colonies, often in Africa. France, England, and Belgium, through their colonies, wielded world power. Hitler realized how Mussolini and the Italians easily conquered Ethiopia despite the efforts of Haile Selassie, Emperor of Ethiopia and the League of Nations.

This story relates how the calling of God impacted the successful lives of a young couple in the 1920s and 1930s. In the 1920s the United States, and the world to a degree, were experiencing the "Roaring Twenties," a period of financial success and frequent celebrations until the sudden Stock Market crash of 1929 brought on the Great Depression. Harold and Mabel left a successful business career to ultimately sacrifice the comforts of their home for lives filled with danger and trials in Ethiopia, Africa.

These entries in the Five-Year Diary reflect Mabel's love story – love for God, love for her husband, Harold, and love for their children: Miriam, Paul, Junior, and Bobby. Included are periods of family separation, poverty, health issues, harsh trials, and an extremely perilous time when Harold was held in chains as a prisoner. Living in rural Ethiopia at this time meant living without modern conveniences such as electricity, running water or indoor plumbing. By God's grace and Divine protection, these struggles saw others' lives changed with victory and joy.

Chapter 1

Following the Call

Harold Blaine Street was born in York, Nebraska, on January 30, 1899. His father, Lindley M. Street, was the president of the Nebraska National Bank in York. Harold's mother, Ida Mae (Hansel) Street, was a housewife. He had two sisters, Maude, fourteen years older, and Ethel, nine years older.

The Street home stressed values, including the need to make a personal commitment to Jesus Christ as one's Savior. Harold made that decision at the age of five, and it directed his entire life.

His mother died when he was eleven years old, and soon afterwards the family moved to Minneapolis, Minnesota, where his father continued in banking. Maude and Ethel assumed the role of being "mother" to Harold during those years.

Harold graduated from West High School and, because of the family resources, was then able to attend Oberlin College in Ohio, where he graduated with a business major. He was part of a quartet that sang in various churches to promote the college and recruit students. While singing in Newark, Ohio, he met Mabel Ellis, his future wife.

Mabel Louise Ellis was born in Newark, Ohio, on February 27, 1899. Her father, John Henry Ellis, was a businessman. Her mother, Kathryn Elizabeth Honenberger, was a housewife.

Mabel grew up in a devout Christian home and accepted Christ as her Savior as a child. She had three brothers, Ned, Rod, and Clyde, and two sisters, Rachel and Katherine.

Mabel attended public schools in Newark and graduated from Newark High School. She continued her formal education at the Moody Bible Institute in Chicago, graduating with a Music Major.

She met Harold when he was singing in her church in Newark, Ohio. Their relationship flourished, and they were married in her church September 27, 1924.

Harold and Mable Street, 1940

After graduating with a business administration degree, Harold began working for Heinz (tomato ketchup) in the early 1920s, and he succeeded in his work in sales and administration.

The Streets lived in the Minneapolis-St. Paul area after their marriage, and Miriam was born August 1, 1926. Paul joined the family on October 3, 1927.

Harold and Mabel remained active in the Alliance Church by teaching and singing in the choir. They had purchased a home and were able to live comfortably. They owned a car, had nice furnishings, and stylish clothes, including a fur coat for Mabel.

Harold advanced at Heinz so that before he was thirty years old, he was named one of the vice presidents of the company. God indeed blessed them, and they were experiencing "the good life" by world standards.

Dr. Rowland Victor Bingham, founder and director of the Sudan Interior Mission, came to their church holding a special missions meetings in 1926. Dr. Bingham quoted Christ's Great Commission from Matthew 28:19–20: "Go therefore and make disciples of all the nations, baptizing them in the name of the Father and the Son and the Holy Spirit, teaching them to observe all that I commanded you; and lo, I am with you always, even to the end of the age" (NASB).

Moved by the message and touched by the Holy Spirit, Harold and Mabel determined to reach out to those without Christ. They talked and prayed that their lives would reflect God's will and bring glory to Him. After considerable deliberation and ongoing prayer, they believed that God was calling them into full-time Christian ministry.

An interview with Hal by Catherine Brandt, for the *Today* publication, captured the moment of their life-changing "call" in her article "Epsilon Alpha," April 1, 1956:

> *"Does God want me to be a missionary?" he asked himself... Wasn't he too old? And what about Mabel and the children ...*
>
> *... Mabel was putting their lunch on the table. He said to her, "Honey, what would you think if I suggested we should be missionaries to Africa?"*
>
> *Mabel looked up from her plate, her dark eyes sparkling, "Why, Hal, I'd say you are right."*

Following the Call

Initially, Harold took some course work at Saint Paul Bible Institute. He later applied to Moody Bible Institute in Chicago. When he was accepted, he resigned his position with Heinz, sold their home, and they moved to the married housing section of Moody with their two children, Miriam and Paul. Harold enrolled in the Pastor's Course which included studying Hebrew, Greek, and many theology classes. Mabel attended Moody as a part-time student and completed the Christian Education major along with her previous music major.

As part of the practical aspects of pastor training, after ordination Harold became the pastor of the First Presbyterian Church in Paxton, Illinois. Paxton is the county seat of Ford County, near Champaign-Urbana, Illinois. This ministry provided a parsonage for the family to live in while Harold preached in the services and commuted to Moody for his final classes in the Pastor's Course. Over the years of study and pastoring, with family prayer about the future, he continued contact with the leadership of the Sudan Interior Mission in New York.

While still living in Paxton in 1932, the local Paxton newspaper contained a little article on the front page that there was a new "Street" in Paxton. The article elaborated that the new Street was Harold Street, Jr., born to Mabel and Reverend Harold B. Street, the pastor of the First Presbyterian Church in Paxton. In addition, father and son shared the same birth date, January 30.

About this time, Harold arranged to give a New Testament to Mabel from Miriam and Paul for Mothers' Day with the words written in the front, "Given to our precious mother with love from Miriam and Paul." This was a New Testament that she cherished and would often use as she spoke to different groups over the years. Below are a few of the notations written by Mabel in her New Testament. (See Appendix B for other notes, quotes, and credits.)

> One task alone, our strength employs;
> No time have we for earthly joys;
> He, who us sought at awful cost,
> Commissions us to seek the lost.
> *(author unknown)*

Psalm 135:14–18 Idols of heathen will perish.
II Peter 3:9 The Lord does not wish for any to perish, but for all to come to repentance.

These verses and many other scriptures impacted Harold and Mabel's lives and ministry for the Lord. Mark 16:15, "Go into all the world and preach the gospel" was increasingly compelling to Harold and Mabel. Sudan Interior Mission served throughout Northern and Central Africa, including Ethiopia in its missionary outreach.

In Acts 8:26–39 the Holy Spirit arranged a special appointment for the Ethiopian eunuch, a royal treasurer of the Ethiopian court, to meet with Phillip the Evangelist. This encounter led the Ethiopian eunuch to accept Christ as his personal Savior, and he was baptized. As an influential government official he did much to help bring the gospel to this region of Ethiopia. This scripture passage and others that stressed the lost condition of those without the salvation of Christ were used to help confirm God's call on Harold and Mabel's lives to serve as missionaries to Ethiopia. Their application to and the acceptance by the Sudan Interior Mission confirmed God's call to them in 1932.

To raise support and transportation expenses for a family of five was substantial and challenging, especially in the time of the Depression. But God! He called, and He would provide. Several churches in the central United States rose to this challenge and made commitments to support them. The task of getting equipment, supplies, and packing was a daunting challenge, but again, "God is able."

In November of 1932 the Streets boarded the ship in New York and began the slow voyage across the Atlantic Ocean to London, England. They finally arrived in Addis Ababa, Ethiopia, Africa, at the end of 1932. They thanked the Lord for safety and traveling mercies.

Harold B. Street and family before going to Ethiopia

The following map of Ethiopia was prepared by the Sudan Interior Mission and used with their permission.

SUDAN INTERIOR MISSION

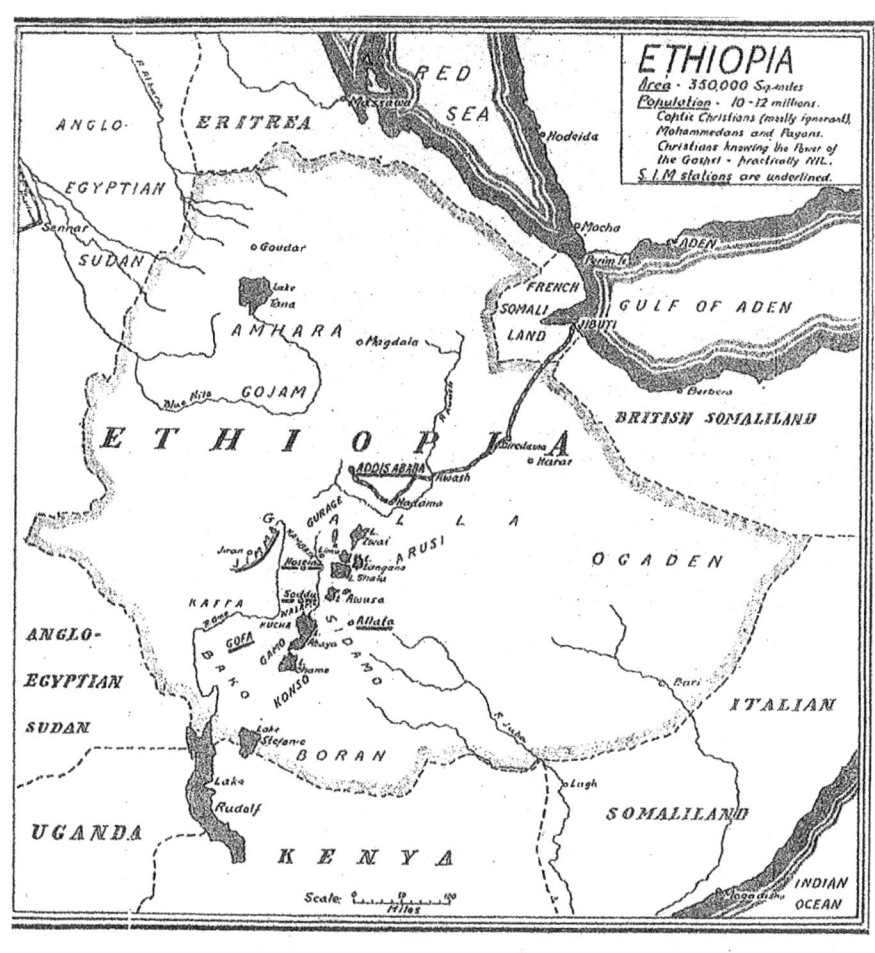

ADDIS ABABA.	Mission Headquarters. Leper Hospital (under construction, 1933). A Printing Office is urgently needed.	ALLATA.	The same as HOMATCHO.
		SODDU.	Hospital work is carried on here.
MARAKO. (Not shown on Map)	In GURAGE District to the W. of L. Zwai.	BULKE.	Capital of GOFA District.

Following the Call

What was Ethiopia really like? Ethiopia lies in northeast Africa on a plateau which is 6,000 to 10,000 feet above sea level, an altitude that ensures a moderate climate even though near the equator. It stays sunny except during the rainy season of mid-June through September, when the rain rarely stops. River gorges cut deeply into the mountains, which reach from 12,000 to 15,000 feet with few passes in the country. This mountainous barrier kept Ethiopia isolated from the rest of the world until the 1930s. The capital of Addis Ababa is in the center of the country, and most roads outside the capital were twisting rocky trails best traveled by mules, camels or pack horses. The Ethiopian Orthodox Church was prominent in the north and central parts of the country, with some influence in the south, where traditional religions mixed with Islam and Christianity. Haile Selassie was the Emperor.

The following chapters of *That None Should Perish, Ethiopia 1933-1937* are the actual entries, transcribed as written, each day by Mabel Street while the family was in Ethiopia from 1933 until August 17, 1937. When the family first arrived in Ethiopia in December 1932, they stayed in the Sudan Interior Mission headquarters building in Furi, Ethiopia, just outside the capital, Addis Ababa.

Chapter 2 covers 1933 and primarily takes place in Addis Ababa and Furi.

Chapter 3 takes place in 1934 in Furi and Soddo about two days travel south by horseback from Addis Ababa.

Chapter 4, 1935, is in Soddo and some in Gamo, two days journey south of Soddo near the border of Kenya and Sudan.

Chapter 5, 1936, takes place in Gamo and Soddo.

Chapter 6 primarily takes place in Soddo and Addis Ababa in 1937 and describes their departure from Ethiopia and return home.

Mabel writes about the S.I.M. Headquarters building in Ethiopia, "Each room has a window and a door to the outside. Our two rooms were at the end of the building. The building was made of brown stone from a quarry which the Lord saw to it was located on the same tract of land. This land was given to the Sudan Interior Mission by Haile Selassie, the Emperor."

Sudan Interior Mission Headquarters, 1933, outside Addis Ababa, Ethiopia

Most of this book is the story of Mabel Street's love and care for her husband and "kiddies," as recorded daily in her Five-Year Diary. Because of the limited space in the diary, she used abbreviations and few sentences to state the highlights of the day. (See appendix B for full names of people, places, etc.). Some dates contain no entry. As one reads her entries, it is obvious to note the many trials the family faced, but also noteworthy are the triumphs that emerged from lives of personal sacrifice in response to the life God had called them to serve and to reach out to others in need.

Mabel wrote the following verses (author unknown) in the opening pages of her small New Testament Bible, given to her 32 years prior:

The restless millions wait the Light
Whose dawning maketh all things new.
Christ also waits, but men are slow and few.
Have we done all we could? Have I? Have you?

Chapter 2

1933, Addis Ababa and Furi, Ethiopia

January 1 – (We arrived here Tues. 12/27/32 in the aft.) Our first New Year's & first Sunday here. A service was held for the natives in the a.m. & a service for us, led by Hal, in the evening; a precious time for all. Miriam continues ill with pneumonia having taken sick 12/24. Dr. & Mrs. Roberts and Mary help so much with her care.

January 2 – Monday & wash day. How interesting to see these Ethiopian men do it! Very different, but with good results. We love this beautiful view; mts. on 3 sides, Eucalyptis trees abound, sunrises & sunsets revealing God, but the people sit in darkness for whom Christ died.

January 3 – Mrs. Horn invited Mrs. Roberts and me to tea today to meet Mrs. Southard, Mrs. Colson and Mrs. Park. The day was spent with the usual duties. What a privilege to live for our Lord in this land which knows of Him, but knows not Him.

January 5 – My sweetheart & I went to Addis today to help "set up housekeeping" again. Bought some necessities including a lamp and Paul's shoes. My, the sights one does see! Tufer acted as our guide and interpreter. We carried canes to push over donkeys, dogs & "what not" if need be. Miriam is improving in health.

January 6 – Mail day – grand. Dr. Roberts allowed Miriam to be up for lunch & part of the afternoon. This siege wasn't as severe as last May's, 'tho she is thin.

These days, we are attempting to learn of the people, their customs & language, tho a teacher hasn't come yet for lessons.

January 8 – What a great time these natives have as they go and come from services examining our beds, babies, toys, etc. Miriam's "mama" doll was the big scare, then attraction to the Jimma chief's wife who then wanted to take it. Junior always gets a smile from them. May the love of Christ reach their hearts & win them.

January 9 – a.m. spent in bed. – "There's a reason." Mr. and Mrs. Horn, Nell, Mary, Florence, (Peg's tooth wouldn't allow her to go) Hal and I went to town and to tea at the Southards'. He was at home. Both of them were very gracious. "Pat is in school in Switzerland." He represents our gov't. here as U. S. Ambassador. Glad we are ambassadors for the heavenly King.

January 10-11 – Fast freight arrived. Unpacked them today 1/11. Nothing unusual recalled these days. The blessing of the Lord and His blessed Presence continues to be our portion and joy for which we praise Him. (Fleas are still going strong.)

January 12 – Fine letter from Katherine. News of Aunt Em's death – Studied alphabet ½ hour. Intermission prayer meeting here. Large attendance, good spirit. Hal did the devotions "Be glad in the Lord." Hal played Karams & I dominoes for relaxation in the eve. Sweet time followed in Bible reading & prayer as we retired.

January 13 – Studied alphabet two hours. Had one hour lesson – Tim Martin. Daddy, Mother & three kiddies walked down to the stream, after; baths followed. Supper on the hill. Early to bed. Junior didn't sleep well, but, "Our God, whom we serve is able."

January 14 – Dick & Audry Sanford spent the day here. Miriam & Paul fell off of Audrey's little horse, but weren't hurt much. Hal helped John E. (Phillips) pack. I spent the aft. writing 5 letters, the a.m.

studying and sewing. Read, wrote to Stubbins, devotions & retired in fairly good season. No rain since our arrival; somewhat cloudy this a.m.

January 15 – (Barbara Jean's sixth birthday.) Sunday – Miriam invited Peggy and John E. to take a walk with her & Paul. They were gone two hrs. so Jr. slept. Hal & I read & Mr. Duff conducted the native service. Before dinner we all sang. A rest & reading & prayer in aft with kiddies. Mr. Horn led the eve. devotions. A "sing" followed. Then a prayer meeting with Zillah, Helen Miller, Mary & me over M's spanking & Ned, Hal & I had a sweet time.

January 16 – To 10:00 a.m. spent marking laundry, etc. (Mon.). In p.m. baked a devil's food cake & helped make ice cream for Nick's birthday (35th?) In the eve tucked in the kiddies & studied Amharic. Praise God for helping with it, as it begins to "soak in" a bit. 3 hours study.

January 17 – Studied 5 hours today in all. Baked four lemon fluff pies (lime) and pie crusts (extra) for tomorrow using whole p.m. My precious lover has been busy with the kiddies & Dr. R's packing. Eve spent with baths, reading, studying & devotions. Slow freight (22 boxes for us in the station today.)

January 18 – Studied 4½ hours including the lesson. Mr. Martin "sprang" a test – 20 words – I missed two. Thank God for His precious helping with the language. No one got more than 18 correct. Glad to be getting the alphabet a bit better. Encouraging. All our slow freight is stored on our porch tonite. Mr. Clarence Duff spoke in the p.m. tonite of his life here. Excellent! Packing & sewing today for Mr. Duff's caravan.

January 19 – Studied hours. This is "Timcot" biggest Amharic celebration of the entire year, I'm told. Mr. Duff & my lover went at 4:30 a.m. to the river, but that part was over & people gone. They returned, ate breakfast & went to the main ceremony. Hal's first attempt at riding from which he suffered most of the next few days and nights, tho he was "game."

January 20 – Ethel & Mrs. Kirk's birthdays. Studied 2½ hours. Tim came not, so no lesson. Mary Virginia Londin came today.

January 21 – We are busy unpacking our slow freight these days. That and language, plus the kiddies fill our days for His glory, we trust.

January 22 – Another Sunday morning. Native service. Nick spoke.

January 23 – More daily dozen, plus language, laundry, etc.

January 24 – The eve. before the Duff party expected to go into the south country. I wanted a little party for my lover's birthday, but know they would be gone so invited Peggy & John E. to come in & make fudge. Had a good (boxing) wrestling match. Who won?

January 25 – Negahdis failed to appear – departure delayed. Native festivals or "hocked" mules seem to be the cause. "All things."

January 27 – Monthly day of prayer. Messrs Horn & Duff went to town to try to find Negahdis, so Hal led the p.m. Sweet time. Just as last prayer was over & we arose the yard filled with donkeys & men so in a few hours Duff, Roberts, John & Jim were on the way to their new homes. No lesson today.

January 29 – Sun., so a service. The Jimma lady was here again today. She enjoyed Junior. Hal, Paul & Nick spent the a.m. calling on a Greek. Mr. Kirk led the evening devotional service – good & timely. "Peace."

January 30 – My own darling's birthday. He & I spent the a.m. in town with the Horns buying a few needed articles. Peggy made a delicious orange birthday cake & Ruth & John T. made pineapple ice cream – so good. We read "The Kneeling Christian" in the evening & balanced books for Zan. Studied two hours. Mrs. Horn gave us a lesson as Tim didn't appear. Daddy put up the children's swing. Natives greatly interested.

January 31 – "Stand still & see the salvation of the Lord which He will work for you today", the verse from the "Promises Box" this a.m. wisely fulfilled after a heated argument between Ruth, Zilla & Digahgo over the baby's laundry for later Digahgo was very sorry and willing to wash. "All things." Studied five hrs. on language.

February 1 – Studied 2¾ hrs. Mrs. Horn taught today – no Tim. I baked pumpkin pies for supper. Turned out well, thanks to the Lord. Father Street's 79 birthday.

February 2 – Pattering rain on the roof awakened us today, so refreshing to hear. News item: Baby girl at Sanfords' at 5 a.m. today. Miriam is finding it hard to stay on top physically these days – tonsils, I fear. Soon I hope the Doctor will return and remove them. Rode [the horse] to Gamalie to prayer meeting. A great time – much fun & stood it quite well. Good p.m. – Dr. Pollack leading.

February 3 – Miriam is all yellow today, bordering on jaundice, I fear. Orange juice, calomel and salts are her diet, primarily.

February 4 – Sat. but no mail this week. Mrs. Bancroft, Christine, Eleanor & Dick Sanford shared our supper under the trees. They entertained us with native songs, etc. Bath nite & to bed in fairly good time, after washing sweaters, hose, etc.

February 5 – Sunday again. We are much in prayer for the native service. A brief one as Tufa was discharged & there was no interpreter. Mr. Horn spoke. John T. led eve. service – "Crosses." Had a good talk after with Mrs. Bancroft. Trust 'twas to His glory.

February 6 – Mon. so was busy with laundry, mending, & studying, etc. Hal spent the eve. with Karams. Miriam is much better. Junior has an ugly cold. Had a good talk with Peg. "Human holy of holies." Hope it helped. Mended hose in evening & studied.

February 8 – My sweetheart had to go to town today, returning after two. After he ate, I went to Kirk's with the Horn's to see about buying some of their things. We didn't get back until nearly six, therefore the day was spent. Miriam had school three hours, which was profitable. I mended Hal's trousers, etc. … Mail today, Maude, Bowden, S. Watts, Jeffries. Good prayer meeting, Mr. Horn leading.

February 9 – Baked Banana cream pies in the a.m. Reviewed Calvert 1st year course (Kirk's) & washed my hair in p.m. Junior doesn't feel so well. Refuses his supper. Hard to get sufficient liquid into him these days. How fortunate were M. and P. to have had such good milk in their infancy! Miriam continues to make strides in her school work. Paul likes it, too. Paul vomited today. Miriam had stomach ache, too bad. Studied 1 hour.

February 10 – Junior vomited during nite. Slight temp. Gave enema. Refuses food. Class this a.m. Couldn't go due to kiddies. Answered Mrs. Colson's dinner invitation for 2/13/33.

February 11 – Hal complains of a bad diarrhea. Very weak.

February 12 – My sweetheart is in bed. So sorry. Sun. again. Short service in a.m. I staid with my lover in eve.

February 13 – My sweetheart is still sick, tho better. We refused, with regret, Colson's invitation.

February 14 – Hal was up a short while today.

February 15 – Prayer meeting. Mr. Horn.

February 17 – Mrs. Colson spent the day here. 2 hr. language class. I didn't get much – being the slow pupil & having Jr. with me. "All things" nevertheless.

February 18 – No mail – "sad story." My lover has a sore shoulder today.

February 19 – Sunday. Very quiet as usual. Spent time reading Bible stories to kiddies. Good eve. service – Hal "2nd Coming."

February 20 – Studied 2 hrs. 6 new words learned. Miriam acts like another tonsil attack is near. Warding (& praying) it off.

February 21 – Studied 2½ hrs. learned 10 new words. Miriam feels better today. Good to be all (of us) on top at once.

February 22 – No studying. Baths. Weary! Paul's eye trouble commenced. Jr. & M. okay. Took walk in p.m. Mail from Katherine, Mrs. Snyder, Alan Craig & Benson's new course.

February 23 – Hal's sore shoulder still persists, but is leaving gradually. Mary Virginia's announcement arrived. I was so glad & relieved, I cried. My, I'm glad she & Katherine are fine now. More birthday card shower from Paxton for me.

February 24 – Hal took Paul to Dr. Pollock this p.m. "Conjunctivitis" is his trouble. This surely is hard on him.

February 25 – Maud's birthday. No mail today. Very tired tonite. Wrote a letter of congratulations to Katherine & a note to Rachael before retiring.

February 26 – Junior's left eye looks a bit red. We are praying God deliver Him if 'tis best. Both of Paul's are terrible now – dear kiddy!

February 27 – Thirty-four years nearer glory! 'Twas a good day, happily spent caring especially Paul & rejoicing together with my lover in Christ. Peggy & Ruth saw to it that I had fresh strawberry ice cream & a 3-layer cake – delicious! Barely looking at language these full days. My lover gave me a beautiful kamona. Precious boy o' mine!

February 28 – Everyone is hurrying around preparing for the Doctor's (& party) arrival tomorrow. Junior's eye seems alright, but he is having loose bowels. Paul's left eye (the 1st) is better. praise the Lord!

March 1 – Dr. Hooper arrived soon after twelve. Ruth & Florence rode out to meet Marion & camp out over nite at "Hywash." Mr. Horn drove out & returned with Dr. & Mrs. Lambie & Miss Robertson soon after lunch. Had a good time listening to God's leading & working for them in evening.

March 2 – Lilly Middleton's birthday. She brot a fruit cake from New Zealand for the occasion – Peggy made ice cream. Helen made chocolate sauce. 20 at the table these days plus Jr. Sweet fellowship

& devotions since Dr.'s arrival. A different tone for which we hungered. I'm so glad & thankful.

March 3 – Dr. L. took all of us (except Jr.) to Furi this a.m. Kirk's are leaving next week for the South. We will then go over there temporarily. Jr. is still troubled with diarrhea. Dr. Hooper gave him sodium sulfate and Epsom salts after saline enema (2 t. salt to 1 qt. water for him) failed. Paul's eyes are nearly well. Pray God to meet our every need in view of Furi. Hal is finishing Dr. L's roof.

March 4 – Today is mail day. None so far this wk.

March 9 – My lover & I rode over to see our new home (Furi). Mary kept the kiddies.

March 10 – Went to Furi & had a picnic lunch in Dr. H's new home on the floor! Freda & Lilly kept Junior at home for me. So kind! Mail day – Zan (round robin) Sara, Mr. Norman, Miss Harris, Voelkels & the A.I.M. bulletin.

March 11 – Spent much of the day in Addis buying supplies for going to Furi. Praise God from whom all blessings flow. How wonderfully He supplies! What a blessing Dr. L. has been to us. Bath day. Washed my hair. Don & Barton's arrived. Kirks left. Junior so happy today.

March 14 –Moved to Furi.

April 1 – Sat. my lover asked me late today what had happened to my dress on the shoulder & to look and see. I did. "April fool!" said he. Ha!

April 9 – Sun. Lilly played for our a.m. service. She & Peggy came over. Hal went to his class at 1:30. Lilly & Laurie went for ride, returning at 5:15. They and I – I rode Dohmoh – went to Akaki – Peggy keeping house for us. After the service, Marion, Flo, Nell, Nick, etc came for [prayer]. We had 10:30 p.m. tea.

April 10 – Junior took cold last Saturday & has felt "under the weather" as a result. Too bad!

April 13 – Thurs. Lilly & Zillah stayed with the kiddies while my Sweetheart & I went to Addis. We ordered a riding suit for me, shopped, etc. Then went to Lambie's to the Thurs. p.m. prayer meeting. Dr. H. led. Laurie had Engeria and Watt for supper. Dreadfully hot! The kiddies cried, it burnt so. The chicken was good, only hot.

Street home, 1933, in Furi, Ethiopia. The length is visible and is one room wide. At the left is the bedroom, living room in center and dining room at other end. At right of house is the little stone kitchen. I have flowers growing all along the little stone wall in front of kitchen. Note the screen doors – an unusual thing out here.

April 15 – Helen brot over a "surprise" from Peggy & Florence – a lovely Easter box – purple & green flowers & cut paper around chocolate, initialed lovely big Easter eggs, each in a dear little paper tinted shell. Thank the Lord – the kiddies will be happy.

Street family, 1933 in Furi, Ethiopia. This was taken about 8 a.m., but even then we are squinting due to bright sun. From 8 a.m. until 5 p.m. we have to wear large sun hats which keep the sun's rays from harming the head.

1933, Addis Ababa and Furi, Ethiopia

April 16 – Easter Sunday. Nel played today and staid until 3 p.m. Praise the Lord for His resurrection. Some day we shall be like Him when we see Him as He is! Hal taught, as usual, then went to Akaki for eve'g. communion service. I staid here.

April 17 – Dr. & Mrs. Pollock called this afternoon. Dr. Lambie gave a talk to missionaries today on health, insects, etc. … Hal & Laurie went over, getting home at 10:30. Miriam prayed that Jesus would make it stop raining so that Daddy wouldn't get wet & he wasn't even damp. How the Lord loves a child and her faith!

April 18 – Tues. Junior still feels some badly, but is much improved. He is walking from chair to chair and occasionally gets a hard fall when his goal is missed.

April 19 – Digago & I went to town this p.m. I had to go to try on my riding coat so did some shopping. The Lord graciously held off the rain until our return at 6:30 p.m. Don & Ruth left today for Jersi-yea. Dr. H. extracted M.'s upper left front tooth.

April 20 – Junior is well again. Miriam had a temp of 103° this p.m. An enema brot it to 100°. I don't know what is causing it – tonsils, sun or what. I've had an a.m. entirely filled by clinic – eyes, cracked feet, etc. Washed my hair. Heavy rains tonight.

May 2 – Dr.'s Lambie and Hooper assisted by M. Berger removed Miriam's tonsils & adenoids this a.m. (1/2 hr. operation.)

May 4 – Zan's birthday.

May 18 – Clyde is 18 today.

May 30 – Memorial Day at home. No thot of it here, but we are glad to be in the place of His choosing for us.

June 14 – Kay's birthday.

Hospital under construction, May 1933, Furi. A noonday service at the hospital with the natives (workmen) who cared to come. There are Indians, Arabs, and Ethiopians. A native boy, Ordufa, is standing by Hal as an interpreter. There is surely a great need here for Christian workers where sin is rampant.

June 17 – Had tea at Hoopers – with all Akaki crowd, etc, due to Mrs. H's birthday. Lois Briggs (25?) birthday also.

July 4 – No sense or thot of holidays here. However, I made potato salad & lemonade to be "sorta" different.

August 1 – Our dear little daughter's 7th birthday. Hooper's came for tea & sent gifts to her. Sanford children are at Mula so couldn't come to her party so their reply stated.

August 4 – Dr. L. took Mrs. H., Helen, the kiddies & me to Akaki about 10 a.m. Hal following in p.m. on Rhoada. Opening session at 4 p.m. of Conference. Good Spirit & attendance.

August 6 – Zan's & Reg's 9th wedding anniversary. "Kins's" glad victory! Blessed time.

August 7 – Mon. Came back to Furi this a.m. Such a blessed time! How precious and gracious our adorable Lord is!

August 8 – The big fight Digago and Gubamudeem all cut up. Giza drunk – blood sacrifice all about his bed, etc. Oh God, break Satan's power in this sin-cursed land. Hal & I are the "ashcans" this week. Miriam & Paul are good helpers.

August 12 – Dreadfully tired tonight. "Under His wings" is enough. Went over to hear Mr. Cain speak. Were disappointed however as there hardly was an opportunity. "All things" tho. Enjoyed the few minutes he did speak. Next Wed. Wyn R. & he leave for home. Dr. & Mrs. L. & Borch-Jensens came over for tea.

August 13 – Hal's (Sun. P.M.) boys gave testimony in the hospital service, followed by Watt and Ingeria (eaten by all except one even tho the fast is on – a good test of their faith) then the class at the hospital in p.m. Mr. Cain spoke in the a.m. service at the hospital.

Uncompleted Hospital Leprosarium, 1933. "Hal oversees work as Supt. here at Furi. Arab masons, Indian carpenters, and native workmen, 40 to 70 to supervise. The Leprosarium will hold 150 patients and a second story for operating rooms. Dr. Hooper and our houses are about 1 long block away, connected by walks."

August 15 – Tuesday Peg & Zillah arrived via plane suffering from Typhus. I must get off some letters soon. Digago came "on duty" today. I'm "used up" but God has supplied strength.

August 16 – Wyn Robertson & Glen Cain left.

August 19 – Bogala with a $5 M.T. Our Father knew our last "bisas" were given to the boys last night. "He careth for you." Praise His Name! "In nothing be anxious," etc. … "Bucha" almost all week has been required to get rested, but "God is faithful." (9 letters off this wk.)

Ethiopian Emperor Haile Selassie to note progress of the Hospital Leprosarium in Furi, 1933. "He was so pleased that he gave $5000 (Ethiopian) toward its completion. In the picture, he is making out the check. Dr. Lambie, our Field Director is next to Haile Selassie. The young prince, a boy of 10, is at the Emperor's left. Notice the servants, etc. … about him. Dr. Hooper (white trousers) is seen and his daughter, Helen – our nearest neighbors. Dr. Hooper will care for the lepers here at the hospital. He is the doctor who removed Miriam's tonsils May 1st. The U.S. Ambassador, Mr. Southard, is talking to Dr. Hooper."

August 20 – God so graciously spoke today in our woman's meeting. "The <u>One</u> Sacrifice – sufficient, Who came to show us the path & light the way home to the Father's home. Ababetch": Then I want Jesus Christ "Ishie". Oh Lord, make it <u>real</u> to him & the others! Hal had a sweet time in the Addis class.

August 22 – Dr. L. brot Mrs. Borch-Jensen, Tredeau, Johannes over. After an hour they returned to Akaki. Hal is going too, to work on Dr's car. A mad dog was killed over there today. Peg & Zillah steadily improving.

August 23 – Hoss Cowser's birthday. Dr.'s car was Hal's employment the entire day, getting home late & very tired. Due to that & Paul's vomitting we didn't go to H's. to p.m. (Bed.)

August 24 – Awakened early – 5 trek mules stolen in nite. I planned to go to Rhoada to the Intermissions p.m. at Akaki. A boy brot a note it was "called off" due to bad road (culvert in repair). Paul is better.

August 25 – John Walter Markham arrived 8:45 p.m. Friday, 7¾ lbs. Before breakfast Ken O. came to say the car was broken down – bolt caused the trouble so Hal & he, Helen & Dr. started to the Day of Prayer. Soon Hal returned with Marion's thotful note & animals. Jr. stayed with Mrs. H. Good day at Akaki for all the others of our family, but Junior cried much of his time.

August 26 – Entire day Hal spent on car – unfinished. Peg & Zillah doing well. Mail from Mrs. Farin, Lilly, Kirks. Eager for mail from Rachael. Bath & hair washing day.

August 27 – A blessed a.m. service at Furi – Hal spoke to men (& Mrs. H. to women). Splendid p.m. class in town. Seemingly one boy was saved there last Sunday. May it be very real for <u>His</u> glory!

August 28 – Hal has gone to try to finish the car.

August 31 – Rode Rhoada to Akaki intermission prayer meeting. Met a truck & had a "grand time." Poor Rhoada! Met Mr. Berman's car on the Akaki road. He insisted on my dismounting & letting Giza take the mule. Had a splendid meet. Peg and Zillah were there – so glad to see them & their splendid improvement.

September 2 – Dr. H., Mr. Russell, Mr. Borch-Jensen & my lover left at 9:30 to climb Furi Mt. Had a delightful day getting home just before dark. I quickly served tea then Mr. B.-J. went to Akaki. Hal & I had dinner with Mr. R. at Hoopers – at 7:15 p.m.

September 3 – Sun. Mr. Russell spoke to the men and I to the women today. Small crowd. The Kalitcha had a sacrifice so had the crowd there. Too bad, but "all things." May they feel the emptiness of their religion. Mr. R. left with Hal in p.m.

September 6 – Hal went to town in a.m. Tea at Hoopers. Dr. L.'s request. Asked us what we thot of taking over a "down country" station – likely Lewis to start Bible school preparations. Prayer meeting in the eve. Dr. L. on Abraham.

September 7 – Dr. Lambie called to Akaki at 5 a.m. Young Mr. Horn arrived at 10 a.m. He and mother doing very well. Eric looks like a full moon, he's so pleased. Queen & King didn't come today – death of Abyssinian High-Bishop. Coming Tuesday. No news yet from Rachael, surely soon now. Wrote to Nony, Mrs. Jahnke, Mrs. Gentry & Katherine. Hal cleaned outer ikabate so it can be moved for H's kitchen. H. H. still sick – vomiting began last night.

September 9 – Ken, Andy & Hal continued work on the kitchen for Hoopers – nearly finished now. I wrote to Given family, Mrs. Crowe, Laura Robinson & Hal to Paxton P. Church. Good letter from Maude. H. Hooper okay now. Junior vomitted twice last nite – oil this a.m. and fine this p.m. Hope it's all over. Each day is full, but blessed walking with the Beloved One.

September 16 – At 3:00 p.m. Dr. Orr died of Typhus. Mrs. Wilson & Mrs. Russell both have it as well. Miriam seems cross. Paul's "shingles" on both ears seem to be drying up. No mail.

September 17 – Sun. Hal preached Dr. Orr's funeral sermon at 11:00 a.m. 400(?) people present. Emitine given to Hal before he went. Miriam's cold is rather annoying to her.

September 18 – Another needle of Emetine for Hal's trouble this a.m. At 9:00 A.M. he went to bed. Miriam is in bed too, today as we attempt to clear up her cold. Dr. H. & Mary B. were to go to Gauldry to relieve in the hospital this a.m.

September 19 – Hal & Miriam spent entire day in bed. About noon Paul got pale and had a pain in his "stomach" so he was in bed all p.m. Sent note to Speedy's not to come tomorrow.

September 21 – Katherine's & Reg's birthdays.

September 23 – Marion had lunch & we spent a happy p.m. tog. Good mail including Aunt M.'s letter and news of 3 boxes coming.

September 24 – Mrs. Gourley's birthday.

September 27 – I invited the whole Akaki & Furi group who came for tea & surprised Hal. 9 years & getting better daily.

September 29 – Mr. Speedy "called for & delivered us" this p.m. at Akaki. P.M. in aft. – lunch at Horns.

October 2 – 4 weeks ago today since Hal's dysentery began. Just getting normal now.

October 3 – Hoopers ate lunch with us. Paul blew out candles & Helen cut the cake. Lambies & Peg supper. All at Hooper's for the evening.

October 4 – Miriam's adenoids operation. Dr. H. & Lois as nurse. Alcohol as chloroform?!

October 5 – Miriam is fine today. Speedy's delightful box & "warakit" came.

October 6 – Ogelsbys staid with the kiddies while Hal & I went to Addis to shop for "down country."

October 7 – No mail. Hal worked on tent at Akaki.

October 8 – One Nagahdie married today – Boys staid all nite at the wedding.

October 9 – Mon. Bocula came at 1:45 p.m. [3 hours & over.] Giza ran off. Digago washed then went to wedding not returning until 6 a.m. What a day! "Unto Him," I am looking. Hal had a good day in Addis, getting home around 3:30. 2 lepers nearly died from mercury ointment.

October 10 – Boys still up in the air. Orderffa's wedding this p.m. All want to go. St James can't come due to a friend's death. Paul, Junior & Bocula vaccinated this a.m. Hal at Akaki – tent making.

October 14 – Marion Walkers & Laurel Grace Speedy's birthday.

October 17 – Zillah's birthday.

November 11 – Armistice Day. Arrived in Soddo just before noon (11 a.m.?). Had a.m. tea at Roberts, lunch at Lewis, supper at Drs. Mrs. Kirk is sending over our Sunday dinner. Mr. L., Dr., & John met us an hr. from the station. Oh, how glad I am to stop trekking, much weight I've lost.

November 23 – Good mail. Ed, Chennault's, Maude, Paxton Christmas mail (J. Adamson), Herb F., Evans (Newark). Filled with preparation for my lover's Dorsey trip. Sleep isn't our portion much these nights with "heavy hearts" for we can't believe Dr's plans to be God's will for us now, but we do want to be wherever He would have us. (What a burden has been ours these last months. May it somehow bring glory to our Lord.)

November 24 – My sweetheart left at 5 a.m. (Rhoada) had to come back after supper. Too bad! Raining. Sewed, washed, had "day of prayer" – I went to a.m. session only. Had a surprise shower for the Bride-to-be Lilly. (Food & funds [$35] given at Roberts home.) Left Jr. in bed. M & P had a delightful time. How we miss our dear Daddy!

November 25 – Father's 63rd birthday. No sleep until nearly morning – time to pray, tho & how needful it is at present. 2 weeks today since we reached Soddu. Wish I could see my Lover-Husband! Miriam asked this a.m. if he'd been gone a week, a month? The rainstorm

& the roof like a sieve. Our tent fly helped, however. Hail at Gamo Hal later told us.

November 26 – Sunday. Mrs. Kirk & Paul had diner here. Paul came in with pains in his thigh & stomach which lasted until late that eve'g. Dr. R thoroly examined him & concluded it was merely an upset stomach so soda then & castor oil next morning. We had supper with Kirks.

November 27 – John's 36th birthday. How fast time goes & how important to be interested only in things of eternal value. Paul got up about 9:30 & is better tho pale.

November 28 – Mr. Lewis says our dear one will be here early tomorrow p.m. A thoro exam by Dr. Roberts this p.m. A very decided functional (seemingly not organic) heart murmur is mine. Well, that is His affair & I'm trusting Him.

November 29 – My Lover came home today 12:30 p.m. accompanied by Mr. Kirk. How delighted we were to get him back again. Made 2 slips for Miriam assisted by Mrs. Kirk, who also made a pair of trousers for our Paul.

November 30 – Thanksgiving Day. Lambie party arrived. Dinner at 6 together at Roberts' followed by a meeting addressed by Dr. L.

December 1 – Gave Junior chlorodyne this a.m. Mother's 57th birthday tho 9 years in glory. I'm glad she is there with these troublesome times. Mr. Speedy in aft. Dr. L[ambie] in eve. Florence, Selma, Lilly & I – quartet sang in the eve'g.

December 2 – Jr. okay today. Mitchells & Mr. Roke came this a.m. at 11 a.m. Mr. Duff came in to ask Hal to speak at the 10:30 a.m. service –impossible then not only because of the lateness of the asking, but because of the 1 ½ hour session with Dr. L. So it has come to this! What of our "heavenly vision", but "He who hath led will lead" & our eyes are unto Him that He may reveal His will.

December 6 – Dr. L examined my heart – fast, but not much sound like murmur now. Conference over this eve with prayer meeting – Dr. L. speaking & male quartet singing. Communion service. Hal, Mr. Duff & boys translated letters to Dejazmatch & Ababa.

December 7 – Dr. L. & party left today – also those from Sidamo. Messrs. Duff & Cowser had supper with us.

December 8 – Sick, am I – vomited 5 times. Such stomach pains & nausea. Mr. Piepgrass had supper (on 9th, not 8th). Mr. Duff left this a.m.

December 9 – Oh, the abdomen cramps. Finally c. oil staid down & acted. In bed all day. Mr. Piepgrass ate supper with us.

December 10 – Weak & aching in every muscle – just so sore, but got up in time to watch Soddo's 1st 10 people baptized. A beautiful sight & so moving! (8 men, 2 women.) Up in p.m. long enuf to go see Kirks. Mail came in by carrier – nice lot for us. Tired, but rejoicing "in Him" tonite.

December 11 – Weakness & aches are leaving gradually. Ohmans, Kirks, Lilly & Mr. Cowser got off. The last leaving about 9:30 a.m. Silver in Junior's & Paul's eyes. Wrote a few letters. Hal has such a cold. Evan's box came.

December 12 – More letters & resting. Removed matter from Paul's right eye a number of times today. Jr's okay. Hal repaired Paul's bed, cleaned girls' house.

December 23 – Read in eve. our Paxton Xmas letters – prepared stockings for kiddies in eve. & took them to Roberts'. Worked so hard.

December 24 – Sun. In eve, Hal & I prepared S. & Mrs. R's Xmas stockings & took them up.

December 25 – Thanks be to God for His unspeakable Gift. Mrs. Duff & Messrs. Cowser & Duff arrived noon. Xmas at Roberts from noon on. How precious to be able to spend day together, but clouded by the thot of what this week holds – my Lover's going. No Xmas pkgs. from family – later?

December 26 – Rushing to get ready for Gamo.

December 28 – All's finished finally, but <u>oh</u> how hard it is to have to be without my sweetheart!

December 29 – Friday. The alarm went off all to soon. Poor Hal couldn't sleep – excited likely plus sore finger & aching head. 5 a.m. my own precious lover is on his way to Gamo. God bless, help, guide, keep, & be all he needs! Prayer day – was at Roberts for prayer & tea from 3 to 4:30 p.m. Dear little Miriam's Pink Eyes are so sore.

December 30 – Another lonely day with tears not always behind the curtains. Baths, straightening rooms preparation for Sun. & many prayers for my darling. Gave chlorodyne to Junior who has loose bowels yet. To bed about 8 p.m.

December 31 – Last day of the year. Wish it were the last day my darling & I were to be separated. Praise God, Miriam's eyes are really better tho annoying enough, I'm sure. Paul's aren't so good. Junior seems alright today. Had S.S. here with the kiddies. Lewis & John called. Laurie arrived in nite at 8.

Chapter 3

1934, Furi and Soddo

January 1 – New Year's Day has no significance in this land. My darling left Fri. a.m. with C. Duff for Gamo, so the kiddies and I are <u>most</u> lonely. We are "looking unto Jesus."

January 1 – At 6:30 the Negadis returned with a letter from my boy. They were tired but safe in Chincha, praise His name! How I miss him! The tears simply refuse to "stay put," but the dear kiddies fortunately haven't noticed them much.

January 2 – Early this morning, we sent off a carrier to Gamo with medicine, shells, "eats" & mail. That helped so much to get my darling's letter last night, but, my, that mountain looks a <u>long</u> way off & he's on the other side of it.

January 3 – Bath day. Miriam & Paul are having sore eyes. Hers are espec. ugly & hard for her to endure, poor little sweetheart. The zinc sulphate is helping, however.

January 4 – Mail came today – still no allowances. It's good that Hal didn't wait longer to get that. The Lord is our Refuge!

January 6 – Sat. Busy with mending, baths, etc.

January 7 – Sunday – spent quietly here alone with the kiddies making them have a happy Sunday, but, "Daddy is not here."

January 9 – Sent things to my sweetheart again today, chili sauce, butter, cookies, canned milk, tom. puree, mail, etc. – Trust it reaches him soon & safely.

January 10 – A carrier brot 2 letters at 4 p.m. from my sweetheart, broken glasses, etc. Prospects for land are bright, but not definite at Shammah, 1¾ hrs. from Chincha. Likely my lover will be coming soon.

January 11 – Peg & John's (Phillips) wedding day.

January 12 – No funds to mail my lover's glasses in today's Addis post. Must pay 1 milk woman today. – He is faithful who promised & my trust is in Him. Yes, about 8:30 Mr. L. came to announce allowances were here. Also oranges for us (31 in all) Laurie left for Addis, having reached here last Mon.

January 13 – Baths, etc. plus preparations for Sunday. The eyes are practically well but still weak & effected by the light. Junior escaped, fortunately.

January 14 – Sunday – spent the day with the kiddies – took a walk between 11 and 12 o'clock.

January 15 – Ned's birthday – 27th one.

January 16 – Nick's birthday. John T. & Mr. Lewis left to be out among the people this week – going northeast. Baboons are annoying to those natives who've requested him to come to kill off what he can. I'm looking daily for my sweetheart now. Dr. & Mrs. Roberts had dinner here this eve. Kiddies were pleased.

January 17 – Made soda crackers yesterday & today cookies, noodles & chili sauce – plus baths & getting things ready to send to my lover in the a.m. I hardly know whether to send them or not since he may be on the way home. "Oh Joy." (Mail today – Kathrine's photo included.)

January 18 – Helped Mrs. L. pack the Gamo bag & sent butter, chocolate, cookies, crackers, noodles, oranges, N.T., notebook & mail to my lover with all my love & prayers. Sewed Paul's bed (2 hrs.) Sent to Addis for supplies (outing included.)

January 19 – (Aunt Clara's birthday) Lois – sugar can't be found (In Gamo?) Couldn't mail my lover's glasses – cash. Timcot – let Bocula & Digago go all a.m. – returned when I told them to – 1 p.m. Will my sweetheart be on the way today?

January 20 – I found it pretty hard today not to have my sweetheart come. Mrs. Lewis & Ruth came over in p.m. John was here a few minutes, noon, telling about their trip in monkey hunting – not much success seemingly. Good letter from Maude (by carrier).

January 21 – Spent a.m. with kiddies reading, memorizing a song & verse & going for a walk, toward Gamo. No darling tho.

January 22 – At noon, Lewis' stable and servants' house burnt, also fences, much grass, etc. – was very hard to extinguish. Horses in our stable now.

January 24 – A precious, long letter from my lover – expecting to be home this weekend. Oh how <u>thrilled</u> I am & the kiddies, too. Our dear Daddy is "all the world" to us. Bath day again. Started to read Hudson Taylor's "Spiritual Secret."

January 25 – Went to Lewis' & Roberts' to share the Gamo news – had "tea" at R's. Baked cookies this a.m. No mail yet from Addis due to Timcot. 10:00 p.m. – at 8 o'clock went to the clinic & there Soddu's 1st native maternity case – a boy – "all is well." Mail carrier – "God is faithful" – $320.00 allowance oh, <u>praise His Name</u>!

January 26 – Tiniest sprinkle of rain about 4:30 p.m. Monthly day of Prayer. My darling has come – oh how <u>glad</u> we <u>all</u> are! And he reached here just after ten a.m. What rejoicing there is! Went (he & I) to the aft pm. at Lewis'– sweet time. C. Duff here for diner in eve – conference over Gamo. Dr. seems unwilling to have the birth in Gamo. May <u>God</u> lead & direct! What a prayer meeting & praise I've had in my heart all day!

January 27 – Saturday. Bath day. Conferences over Gamo, needed supplies, mail, etc, etc. <u>So good</u> to have my dear one.

January 28 – Sun. In a.m. Hal attended service. After a p.m. rest, etc. all of us took a walk toward Gamo with my darling pointing out all the road. How good 'twill be when we all go home there.

January 29 – Grandmother's 83 birthday. Weary today. My sweetheart says "Too long a walk yesterday." I think so, too, but I'm glad we went, nevertheless. In late aft. I baked my lover's & Junior's birthday cakes. A camel at 5:30 with 2 beds. "I'd give a cookie to know where they came from," says our dear Daddy, but we thanked <u>God</u> for them.

January 30 – The birthdays today. I made chocolate bars, iced the cakes, lemon fluff pie, etc. in a.m. Had whole station (5 kiddies & 9 adults) here for 4 p.m. tea. Such a happy day & I'm so glad our Father allowed us to spend it together. Hal is drawing up Soddu hospital plans these days. How good the beds felt last night. "Before they call, I will answer" proved again in this case.

January 31 – Busy getting things "lined up" for the Negadis to take to Gamo early in the a.m. My lover is rushing around & tired. Let Digago go. Bath day! Doesn't matter much [that I'm tired] as my sweetheart is here. No mail today.

February 1 – Negadis got off this a.m. & while there's still plenty to do, there isn't the rushing necessary like the last time my dear one had to leave. He worked until 11:30 p.m. on the hospital plans, but completed them last nite – today he's copied Walamo notes & spent the day with us. To bed soon after eight.

February 2 – Mail today – nothing special. Awakened at 3:20 a.m. so turned off the alarm. Called my darling – awakened Bocula and at 5:00 (or a bit before) my own dear heart had to break away from us and go. How precious he is & how we long to be together & want these days to fly in the meantime. God bless, guard, guide & keep him. Wrote to Mrs. Jefferies this p.m. Kiddies & I all well.

February 3 – The kiddies & I did the cleaning today. I spent 1 hr. in class & 1½ hrs. in study. Baths, too & I'm "quivering" with weariness. Rain around 3:30 p.m. or so. Thunder etc. Tried to study in eve – too weary – to bed at 8:30. God bless my darling – how I miss him. He's due in Shammah.

February 4 – Sunday & Daddy isn't here – God bless him. Digago left for Addis at 7:30. Bocula took Coso so Iraba & I did the work with M. & P. caring for Junior. M. & P. both have colds so feel "ugly." Nap in p.m. – copied Walamo notes – went for a half hour walk – got supper – more notes – wrote to Hal – read & to bed at 9:30. Tired!

February 5 – D. L. Moody's birthday. Prayed for the Founder's Week Conference. 1 hr. in class. 1¾ hrs. study. So fatigued had to stay in bed until time for class & 2 hrs. in afternoon. Gave chlorodyne to Junior today. P. & M. still having ugly (tho improving) colds. Read (after studying) & went to bed before 9 p.m. No negadis with mail from my lover.

February 6 – In a.m. made cookies, went to class & took care of the kiddies – Took Junior to clinic – navel has a bit of pus "likely" infected insect bite. Dr. says give him chlorodyne twice today – a bit better tonight – he slept 3½ hrs. I knotted a comfort (top washed) wrote to Mrs. Ruth Carlson, Alga Allin & Christies & to bed about 9:15. No word from my darling yet. Soon, I hope.

February 7 – About 4 p.m. my darling's negadis arrived. How eagerly I tore open his letter & devoured it. What a terrible trip down he had. May God take away the cold & meet him these first, trying days for His glory! Cut all the kiddies' hair & washed it. Baths.

February 8 – Made a chocolate drop cake this a.m. for my lover – hearts yesterday. Wrote letters, knotted two comforts yesterday & today, the covers of which had been washed. Mail from Trout, Bowden, Horn, Davis (Jimma), Zillah, Nina Briggs, E. Jones (Birthday greetings to Hal). Wrote to my Boy – busy getting things ready to go to him in the a.m. Mr. Smith arrived – leaves for Sidamo.

February 9 – Concluded the letter to my sweetheart & finished packing his things. Tried to persuade Mrs. L. to get the iron off quickly for our kitchen before he goes to Sidamo Mon. for 2 weeks trip with Mr. Smith. Wrote to Sara & Rachel – mail off tomorrow to Dr. L., Kirks, R. Carlson, Olga Anderson, Mrs. Christie, Mrs. Salis, glad for that, but oh what a pile of "unanswered" letters yet! Headache tonite – using my eyes too much, I fear. Kiddies all well again. To bed soon past 9: 30 p.m.

February 10 – Sat. – a.m. kiddies & I cleaned house, had baths, washed woolens. Dinner over kiddies to bed for naps, my bath, rest & reading. Junior doesn't seem quite well today – cross. Miriam's & Paul's colds are gone. Mr. L. bought metod & iron in town this p.m. John's horse was poisoned this eve.

February 11 – Sun. Spent day with kiddies – thot so much of my darling. Sweet time communing with my Lord. Oh that I might be, truly, faithful to the praise of His glory! Mr. L. came to tell us to come to communion service there (with native believers) at 5:30. Hurried supper & went. (Jr. better tonight – enema & oil this a.m.). Met carrier with Maude's sweet package & Dr. L's letters. Dr. S. <u>might</u> go to Gamo (Joy!) Wrote to my lover in eve. Bed at 10 p.m.

February 12 – Iron was taken to Gamo for watt-bute roof as well as metod this a.m. John sending it down. Messrs. Lewis & Smith left for Sidamo. I sewed ½ hrs. mending on Selma's machine at Roberts this forenoon. Rest, wrote to Don & Ruth, made biscuits. Rain & hail & torrents thruout the house from 4:30 to 5:30. Am <u>I</u> tired looking after it all & achy. Jr. better. In eve wrote to Peg, Zillah & a note to Mr. Horn as carriers are to take sewing machine to A.A. for repair. Retired 9:15.

February 13 – Prayed for food today, not expecting a feast, but the Lord sent natives with guineas and fresh ripe peaches (which were unknown to all at this station previously). Praise His Name! Spent all day working constantly drying out trunks, boxes, clothes, etc. after yesterday's "deluge." Helped see the large washing was done – So weary, but "glad in Him" tonite. Jr. better after nap.

February 14 – Bath day again & and work of that day. Valentine Day. How I'd love to be with <u>my</u> <u>lover</u>, but may God make that possible in His own time and way. The iron should reach Shammah some time today.

February 15 – Mail came from Addis & my darling today. How glad I always am for the latter especially. The Lord is undertaking in Gamo. Praise His Name! $2 for Hal's and my birthdays from Maude, 2 hankies for Jr. Miriam & I were vaccinated this a.m. Another guinea & bananas bought today. Wish my lover could have some down there. Wrote to girls today. Drizzling rain tonite. Tired so must get to bed soon – it's now 9:30 & I want to write letters, but must stop or "pay up" dearly for it tomorrow. God <u>is</u> love & I'm proving Him.

February 16 – I mended my sweetheart's trousers, got things together to send off to him by special carrier early tomorrow. Wrote to Miss J. McLean's S. S. Class, Aunt Minnie & the family Lillian Olson & my own lover before retiring at 9:45 p.m.

February 17 – Bath day – hair washed (mine) also gave Mrs. Lewis my blue dress, hat & shoes, also 2 pr. new bloomers toward her home-going. Sent my sweetheart's mail & other things this a.m. Men who wouldn't stay in Gamo & work returned bringing a sweet Valentine love-letter to me. More prayer necessary – Gamo men don't want to work. We're looking to Him to meet us.

February 18 – M's & my vaccinations have both "taken" slightly. Spent this Sunday as most others as "unto Him," endeavoring especially to enrich the children's lives with Bible stories, songs, etc. Had sweet time in prayer while they were in SS. (Luis') & Jr. & I went to Roberts before supper. One man came who wants to go tomorrow to Gamo to work so in eve. I wrote a letter to my lover.

February 19 – Sent off Tesima to Gamo with mats, Toms, & my letter – 4 other men accompanying him. Late this p.m. 2 more came who said they are leaving in the morning. The Lord is working & we need to keep looking to Him to supply money & materials, etc. "He is <u>able</u> and <u>will</u>." Mending nearly all day – much yet to do. All well!

February 20 – Usual duties – plus sewing on Selma's machine 1 hr. & a quarter this a.m. Further mending in aft. & a letter to Zan. – One to all the Adamson's in eve'g. The vaccination is prickly & itchy, but not bad. Miriam's is almost all over – there'll not likely be any scar from it, tho it "took" very slightly. [Iraba] did the washing well today.

February 21 –Such terrific back pain, had to go to bed right after kiddies were tucked in, but not to sleep very well for I couldn't get relief. Rokes & Mr. L. got in today. Bath day.

February 22 – Had Rokes for lunch. Kiddies were so nice while they were here. Their Donald was circumcised this p.m. – all right now. Mail from Hazel, Gordon, Allan, Mrs. Wright. I made a few things to send to my lover in the a.m. – Same old kink tonight, but not so severe. I've just had a sweet time writing to my darling.

February 23 – Prayer Day. Spent the a.m. mending and communing with my Lord. In p.m. at Lewis' for the prayer service – sweet time. Wrote to Ethel Johnson – Paxton also in a.m. & Hazel. Sent off my sweetheart's mail, etc. by regular postman this morning. Made some tomato preserves for "good kiddies."

February 24 – Made date cake and snow pudding, gave baths, besides mending, etc. Paul had two jiggers & I one which we removed. It seems so long since we had any word from my lover. The postman should reach him tomorrow with our things & mail. Lillie & Laurie did not come, as expected by Lewis' & all. Mar. 2nd is Lillies' birthday.

February 25 – Sunday, and as breakfast was finished, in came a boy with birthday letter & love from my own dear sweetheart who'd hoped to come himself, but couldn't. How we'd loved to have seen him! Letter helped. Went to bed with hot water bottle & the kiddies praying for my terrible back ache at 6:45 p.m.

February 26 – Rokes left this p.m. for home. Hot day! Made a cake so that the kiddies wouldn't be disappointed not to have it tomorrow. "Devil's Food" – wish my lover could have some, too. Sewed from 3 to 5 p.m. at Selma's machine. In eve. wrote to Irie Welch. Devotions & to bed with hot water bottle again at 9 p.m. The pain isn't quite so intense tonite.

February 27 – The Lord has graciously blessed & used all these here to be so kind to me all day long. Lillie & Laurie came at 9:15. All had a.m. tea & Addis news at Roberts. Mrs. L. sent lovely box of candy early this a.m. & had surprise tea for me (cake, candies 'n all) in p.m. Roberts sent two fine linen towels. Lewis' – 9 bars laundry soap. I'd made a devil's food cake & had it & candles here at noon for the kiddies benefit. They were so sweet singing Happy Birthday early this a.m. The Lord was precious. My lover only was lacking & what a lack! How I missed & long for him only. Wrote a 2½ hr. letter to him in evening – A.A. news mostly.

February 28 – And Feb. is gone! Miriam coughed so hard most of the nite, I kept her in bed half of today. Gave oil – vomited at noon. Much improved tonight. She lost her 5th baby tooth today. Paul & Junior are well – tho they, too, have some cold. I slept only 2 hrs. last nite – rained easily from midnight on, but I had to look after the "drips." The Lord has helped me thru the day, however, remarkably well. Laurie's appendectomy successful this a.m.

March 1 – Precious love-letter from my sweetheart about 9 a.m. How I long to see his dear face these days! Gov't. mail at noon – Eric, Maude, Crowell (<u>Praise</u> <u>the</u> <u>Lord</u> – a $50 check!) Bill Rogers. Andersons will start in a wk or two for Goffa & Forsberg for Gamo. Ohmans (& possibly Kirks) expected to leave yesterday for the W.S. Sent for Dr. R[oberts] this a.m. Miriam was so pale & nauseated. "Keep in bed all day – light diet – much liquid – I'll see her tomorrow." She's better tonite. Paul has badly infected big toe – 2 jiggers – toe purple. Junior & I all right. Made a cake – got meals (Boc. sick) & took care of kiddies.

March 2 – Lillie's Birthday. Miriam was up most all day & feels pretty well. Paul's jigger [chigger] infection is a mess – Lois dressed it for him. (I) removed a jigger from one of Junior's toes too. Letter from Dr. L. stating Mary B. "may be down soon." Sewed 2 hrs. at Roberts – making "shorts" for Junior. Wrote to Eric & sent size of shoes & order for hose. Wanted to write to Mildred & P. B. but it's too late tonite to do that.

March 3 – Sent Bocula & Irabo to town so I got lunch, made chocolate pie for the Lewis', 2 pumpkin ones for us & chocolate pudding for tomorrow (Sun.). Gave baths, washed woolens & my hair, had a rest (so tired). At 4 p.m. Mrs. L. came to invite us for lunch – whole station – to surprise Lillie in honor of her birthday yesterday. Home at 7:30 after prayers.

March 4 – Usual Sunday, but oh how my heart ached & longed for my lover! Tears won't stay put, but the dear kiddies were spared from seeing them.

March 5 – Studied 3 hrs. 40 min. on Walamo copying notes & studying alphabet. Tired tonite.

March 6 – Wrote to Miss E. Seibenheiner in aft. & copied language notes 3 hrs. today. Nothing else accomplished, however. "Looking away to Jesus" to sustain & provide. Dear kiddies so sweet & good these days.

March 7 – Mended hose for my lover – copied notes (Walamo 2 hrs.) baths. Paul's sweet confession of Christ as he went to bed so he'd be ready to meet our adorable Lord. Miriam's sweet growth in grace noted in her prayer. May God lead them on richly in Him.

March 8 – Mail (good, large one) came in a.m. & was greatly enjoyed (except one which caused me to look away to <u>Him</u>). God so sweetly sends tokens of His favor & I praise Him for them all. Prepared things for Gamo & wrote a lengthy letter in evening, getting to bed late all these nights.

March 9 – Weary indeed even in morning – had to go to bed 1½ hrs. in forenoon & equally long in p.m. Wrote a partial letter to Mildred & P. B. & the church. Mail left today, so I didn't attempt to finish it (unknown previously by me). Sewed at Rs. 1½ hrs. Had 3 fish!! for supper. Lord's miracle using the R's to give it to us.

March 10 – Baths, usual Sat. cleaning & Sunday preparations. About 2:30 Abi (Nick's boy) came with a letter from my darling telling me he'd be here next Thursday. Thrilled!

March 11 – Mr. L. came in (in a.m.) with the news that Ruth & Don were at Durome & would be here tomorrow for a few days. Mrs. L. ill.

March 12 – Had Lillie & Laurie for lunch. The Davis[es] came about noon & came on in to see us (as we ate our soup.) Few articles came from A.A. (– 4 carries) including Hal's shoes.

March 13 – In a.m. my darling leaves for home. Lord bless him! Had Ruth & Don to lunch (tho wondered what to feed them. The <u>Lord</u> provided, of course). They left about 3 p.m. – had 1 hrs. rest, looked after outgoing mail which carriers took to Addis (Tuesday) 11 letters (to be stamped there), dampened laundry, made cookies for Roberts' "joint" supper, got all ready & went to Rs.

March 14 – My lover is on his way to me today. Baths – preparation – usual routines. Ruth & Don left this p.m.

March 15 – At 10:45 good ol Pax galloped in carrying faithfully my sweetheart. What a precious day of fellowship we've had together. Thank the Lord for him.

March 16 – My lover and I figured out an A.A. order this a.m., plus other duties. Bocula took Coso, so since I was cook, I'm tired indeed. Tonite Balacho's gone, too.

March 17 – Mrs. Lewis' heart bad – in bed yesterday & today so this a.m. I sent them half of our cake & a pan of cinnamon rolls. Baths – Sun. preparation, etc. Hal went to town in a.m.

March 18 – Such a lovely Sunday with our little family complete! In p.m. Daddy took Miriam & Paul for a walk while Jr. & I prolonged our rest.

March 19 – Laurie & Lillie had lunch here.

March 20 – Dr. & Mrs. Roberts for lunch.

March 23 – Selma & Lois for lunch. (Want to have everyone for a bit of fellowship with our dear Daddy.) House like a sieve & dreadfully damp. Sharp pains for me – rheumatism??

March 24 – Hal took M. & P. to town as he had to go to register (some checks) a letter to A.A. After their return Junior was taken for a ride on Pax with Daddy. Pax slipped in the mud & Daddy & Junior did likewise. Uninjured, thank the Lord. Retired at 8:30, to rise in 10 min. & call Dr. R[oberts] with Hal in dreadful agony. Dr. gave atropine needle & then a morphine one. Gall stone – poor, dear lover!

March 25 – Quiet Sunday looking after my own darling who had to stay in bed. Much better in evening. Camels came with Andersons, Davidsons, Forsberg "Ika" & P. B.'s box – soap & sugar for us. What a lot of excitement & many nice things. How we thank our loving Father for His loving care for us as seen in this token from Him!

March 26 – My lover directed the thatching grass preparation today & feels very much better. (Such suffering as he experienced Sat. night, I never saw before – his whole face was marred and misshapen from it.) I was quite "used up" all day today – reaction, no doubt.

March 27 – Wash day – usual routine. Had Mr. Lewis & John in for lunch. Junior has a swollen gland – "to bed" said the "Hockens." Little spots on his face – measles, he thinks. Junior plays & feels well, but is pale – no extra temp.

March 28 – Dr. R. says "Yes, measles." Bath day.

March 29 – 3 carriers arrived – one brot Paul's shoes & his & Hal's hose – all so nice. Dates, soda, etc (thru Lewis) $10-12 in all. Junior has 1 degree extra, temp today, but feels fine.

March 30 – Phyllis Katherine Ellis born today. Prayer Day (Mrs. R. sent lovely hot cross buns.) Hal rode out to meet the Andersons. Mr. F. stayed over a day with Peg & John. I baked a date cake – made chocolate pudding, wrote to Mrs. Congram, looked after Junior, etc. & attended p.m. in aft. Hal went in the evening – sweet afternoon meeting. Easter greetings from Florence. Sweet baby dress & letter from Zillah & Mrs. Annan.

March 31 – Mr. Forsberg due today. Will stay with us. Hal rode out to meet him returning about 1 p.m. or thereabouts. They decided to leave Mon. sending Negadis today. Very busy with his coming, Sunday preparations, Junior's measles, heavy hail storms, leaky roof, packing, etc. & went to bed with a nervous hysteria – too tired to be able to stop crying.

April 1 – Easter – Praise Him for His glorious triumph! So very tired today – could hardly drag out of bed, but had to. More hot cross buns, couldn't eat until nearly 9 a.m. as Negadis left today instead of last night. Mr. Forsberg then went to native service. Hal prepared communion message for this eve. He feared another attack when in eve. meeting, but it wore off. To bed about 10:30 p.m.

April 2 – Alarm at 3:30 & about five a.m. my lover got away. None can know how hard it was to see him go & to face these next few weeks or so without his help & care. Physically the toll is such a heavy one & I could hardly manage the last few weeks he was gone last time, but there's no alternative so come what may, the Lord alone will have to undertake. To bed at 6:40 p.m.

April 3 – Junior looks "peaked" today but is happy & playful for which I am so thankful. I'm not so nervous or quite as tired today either. Sewed at R's – yesterday & today worked on 3 sheets & 12 muslin napkins. In the evening I wrote to my own darling one. To bed about 9:30. (The Negadis have gone, so hope will be able to sleep tonight – Lillie is better.)

April 4 – Spent much of this day in bed, too weary & achy even to read, 'tho I wanted to & attempted it – without success. In p.m. gave baths, rinsed out a few clothes & for Daddy made a few cookies.

April 5 – Still spending most of the days in (or on) bed, attempting to relieve a few aches & weariness. Good mail from the U.S. today. I'm eager for mail from my darling. Junior still has measles.

April 6 – Paul soaked his foot in hot water all day. My sweetheart's letter (brot by returning Negadis) came about 5 p.m. How glad I was to learn he'd reached there safely & not too tired. We do hope, before long, these days of separation will be ended. I need him so much these days. Still worn and weary, I am. Wrote to B. Fox, Perdue, Bentley & Anna Evans (Japan.)

April 7 – Paul's foot <u>much</u> improved, but he continued soaking it all forenoon. The "red streak" is all gone & the toe is soft now – all came from a nail in his shoe. Yesterday & today saw 54 pads (mine) made. Each bit helps. M. & P. helped. Baths & a fair rest, too, in the afternoon. I surely am not much good these days, having to lie down every little while. "All things."

April 8 – Ethiopia's Easter. The great fast ends. Let Bocula & Irabo "off" after dinner for the remainder of the day. Went to see Davidson's & Anderson's before they should leave tomorrow. Paul's foot is nearly well. Jr. continues with measles & wasn't quite as happy as usual, 'tho not terribly cross. We miss our dear Daddy so very much.

April 9 – Finished first pad-making (76 in all, done.) Made date rocks and shared them with the Andersons, Davidsons & Lewis & hope to send some if there's room to my lover & we'll have a few for us. Mr. Forsberg's box is to go by carriers in a.m. so I'll write more to my lover tonight for them to take. Laurie's Negadis failed to appear, so they are still here.

April 10 – About 10:30 a.m. Andersons & Davidsons left for Goffa. 4 carriers left for Gamo this a.m. with one of Mr. F.'s boxes. They also took my Sun. & Mon. letters to my lover. In eve., I wrote a bit more to my darling to send off in the morning.

April 11 – The Negadis with 2 mules, rugs & Mr. F.'s "ika" left at 9 a.m. taking ink and a letter to my sweetheart. I finished 3 sheets today, gave baths, did a little washing & had school. Junior's rash has nearly all gone. He's pale and a bit cross & misses being outside, I think.

April 12 – Such a precious letter came about 5 p.m. from my lover! Paid Lewis for food (A.A.) $10-12 & also redeemed the $8.00 from the 1st Presb. Church to send to Eric toward our A.A. food order. Wrote to Lena Shisk, "Win-Some" class Ethel's church & Maude, Ethel, & Father.

April 13 – The Lord has made this a good day. Little Junior spent ½ hour playing out in the sun & how he enjoyed it after being indoors 2½ weeks. Paul acts like a cold is coming on – I wonder if it is a measles forerunner. (Wrote to Kath. & Rachael, Mrs. Horn & Francis Watts Johnston. (– asking about Junior's carriage.) (The mail of last week was held over so all this should leave tomorrow.)

April 14 – Sewed (made 2 sheets & 2 boys aprons besides mending several things) all a.m. Baths in p.m. & got supper as Bocula didn't get back from market until 5:30. Went to bed at seven, so full of aches & weariness. Dr. examined me to ascertain whether or not it was safe for him to go on a vacation. He and Mrs. R. are going Mon.

April 15 – Sunday – a quiet day. In a.m. I wrote to Nony & her family. Had a rest in p.m. Mrs. Lewis walked over – the first she'd been out for many weeks. A precious letter came about 5 p.m. from my lover (the young Negadis got in). How glad I was for it! In evening I wrote to him. Junior is out of quarantine. M. & P. well.

April 16 – Sewed 2 hrs. made 5 napkins, 1 sheet, finished 3 aprons (boys) this a.m. Rested, then wrote letters in the afternoon and eve. To Gentrys, G. Kilgore, Adells, & Frettis. I must get my pile of unanswered letters down! Dr. & Mrs. R. left for 2 wks vacation. Paul has a bad cold & Miriam went to bed with a sore throat. I've been treating them all day. Jr. & I pretty well.

April 17 – Wash day. Helped hang & remove clothes. Planted 2 front flower beds. Sewed, (mended) 2 hrs. at R's. Buna was called for Danyah at noon. Miriam & Paul both have colds. Paul's is especially miserable. Helped them begin letters to our dear daddy this aft. I wrote this evening.

April 18 – Mended, helped kiddies with Daddy's letters, wrote Aunt Clara & Grandmother. Took care of the "inside" rain, gave baths. Kiddies all have bad colds. To bed at 10 p.m. Sorry to be so late as I've been tired all day, but couldn't get thru any sooner.

April 19 – More letters written. P. B. & Mildred, their church monthly & to my lover. The Negadis leave early in the a.m. with their food from A.A. for mail didn't arrive today.

April 20 – Negadis left for Gamo this a.m. Ethel's fine box came – so full of nice things. Dr. B. phoned Mr. L. from Sidamo – will be here next Fri. I sent for Hal in tonight's letter which Tiginia will leave with in the a.m. 17 letters in today's mail – $20 U.S. & $173.43 Jan. allowance, including $110.43 for the kiddies. Wrote to Hal, Mrs. Horn, Mrs. G. Grayson, Zillah, Annans, Ethel, Tired!

April 21 – Gamo post left today. Also mail prepared for A.A. carriers to take early tomorrow a.m. Wrote to Bartons, Hoopers & Fern Burns, Horns. Baths & cookies plus regular living. Very tired. Retired by 6:30, kiddies in bed by 6. Rainy so nearly dark by then. Didn't sleep much last night – too keyed up & weary. (Did the same this night.)

April 22 – Sunday

April 23 – At about 9 a.m. Roberts returned from a week of rest. Dr. examined me about 11:50, or so, & as I left their house, my darling & Nick were coming up the road – joy, oh joy! I could hardly believe my eyes! How happy we are to have him back again.

April 27 – Prayer Day. Dr. Roberts wouldn't let Hal ride out in the rain to meet Dr. B[ingham] & group, due to his slight attacks recently. Dr. B. didn't get in until 2:30 p.m. nearly. Had sweet evening meeting together. Peg, John, Zillah & Mr. Duff reached here at tea time. John Truwin's birthday.

April 29 – Sunday – p.m. & even'g meetings only. I was too far spent to go in aft., but enjoyed the evening.

April 30 – Talked with Dr. B. until 11:30 p.m. Hal & I – sweet time together. Communion service for all in evening. Messrs. Roke & Mitchell left.

May 1 – Dr. Bingham & Dr. Hockman left soon after lunch. Their visit has brot rich blessing.

May 2 – Nick returned to Shammah in a drizzling, foggy rain about ten a.m. How glad we are our darling Daddy is to stay here now.

May 5 – Had a "station" supper in honor of Mrs. Lewis' & John T.'s birthdays. To bed, after writing a letter or two, rather late.

May 6 – Mrs. Lewis' birthday – Sunday. Many natives to see Selma & Mrs. L. the last time for a year or so.

May 7 – My darling had another quite severe attack this eve. So thankful it didn't last quite so long. Peg, Zillah, Lewis' & Selma left today. Much prayer follows them.

May 9 – Bath day, mending, etc. Billy (the horse) got back about 4:30 from Duomi.

May 10 – In bed (& slept) much of the day. How thankful I am to have my darling here to care for all of us! The Lord is good to me!

May 11 – Made lemon fluff pies (one for J. Truwin & Jr. & one for us) & a banana cake this forenoon. After a good rest, mended – wrote to Borch-Jensens in p.m. My lover had another slight attack last night so he didn't get to sleep at all until 3:30 a.m. (No mail today.)

May 13 – Sunday. Fewer attended services, but 'twas a good opportunity to see who comes because of interest in the Lord rather than people. Station supper here – unexpectedly.

May 14 – My precious lover had another terrible attack last night. Something must soon be done. May <u>God</u> direct in everything is my prayer!

May 18 – Ruth Lewis' 2nd birthday. Began a letter to Clyde – unfinished. Wrote others, however, to leave in a.m. Messrs. Graham & Smith arrived.

May 19 – Donald Roke's 1st birthday. Smith & Graham lunched with us.

May 20 – Sunday. John & Johannes ate here at noon. Shirley Reynolds is "one" today. Quiet & restful day. (Kostner Ave. box came.) Had "station" supper & service at Rs'. To bed rather late for dear kiddies.

May 21 – Wrote letters for Tues. carrier to take. Late in p.m., my lover went to town. Pax stepped in a hole, throwing my darling. (Pax turning a double summersault.) That night brot "Shama chills."

May 22 – How peaked & worn my sweetheart looks & is today – in bed. Headache, but no chills – salts – hope he's better tomorrow. Smith & Graham left.

May 23 – Baths – jiggers (of which there's an abundance these days), school, etc. My sweetheart's so pale today. Stormed all p.m. – Out of the storm at rest time.

May 24 – Mended – school for kiddies & baked. Washed my hair & was so tired I could hardly finish it – slightest exertion uses me "all up." Mail, $10 from Aunt Minnie "for 2 cows." (My darlings A.A. trip.)

May 25 – Prayer Day – a.m. & p.m. sessions together. Wrote to Evelyn Marlott, Paxton church & Clyde. Made cookies & peach butter for Mal & Nick. Paul has an ugly bad cold. All taking soda & lime.

May 26 – Miriam's cold is developing, I fear. Bocula & Balacho failed to return from market until driven home by storm (6 p.m.). <u>White</u>

potatoes (chips) for supper (Mrs. R.) – Hal & I made them. They were so good.

May 27 – Sunday. All but Daddy dear have colds. He went, as usual, to the a.m. service. I taught the kiddies their S.S. lesson, etc. Very damp, foggy & cold – had to light the heater. Supper at Roberts. Junior didn't rest well at nap or night due to "stuffy" head. My lover had to take Atropine during the night. (Sun.)

May 28 – Stayed in bed until 10 a.m. from my cold, – tired and sleepy, but gave Miriam & Paul their school work from my bedside. The "pup" came – thrills! Also letters from Duffs, Zillah & Davies (the later, including 5 M.T. Thank God). I immediately wrote to Zillah, Peg & Ruth D. also to Mrs. Showers & Voekkels this p.m. Bed at 10.

May 29 – The dear kiddies are so happy with "Pru." They can hardly eat their meals. Wrote to Asla Thompson, Don & Margaret, Adela Holms & Ned.

May 30 – Wrote to Florence Walsh, Ruth Cobel, Sarah & Arthur. (Bath day – washed out few woolens after.)

May 31 – Dr. Roberts birthday (31) so had "tea" & mail there.

June 3 – Station supper here. Children's Day at home. Noticed "spots" in Paul's hair & on his neck – cut off hair & applied merc. oint[ment]. Praying he may be spared last year's trouble.

June 6 – Mr. Lewis & John Phillips arrived about 2:45 p.m.

June 8 – Mail today. Zan's letter only thing of value. Returned Hal's letter to Mr. Crowell & S.S. Times article.

June 9 – Johnnie Phillips went home this a.m. after having a tooth filled, heart examined, etc. My darling worked so hard on the davenport today, that he is completely worn out tonight. Sent off mail, including articles to S.S. Times & "E.C." Paul's head is practically clear of "spots," praise the Lord! Dusida seriously ill – "relapsing fever?"

June 10 – "Fathers' Day." The kiddies gave their dear Daddy a box of caramel, coconut fudge. Had supper at R's., Dr. bringing a message & discussion, after, on Satan – good!

June 11 – Terribly foggy day. My heart was "acting up" yesterday & today. Tried to mend & help with schooling, but couldn't do much. Hal & I made baby announcements.

June 12 – Wrote to Bescilla Burkard. In evening my darling and I completed the baby card announcements (as much as possible before its birth) & studied materials for the kiddies' schooling.

June 13 – Dr. & Mrs. Roberts 3rd wedding anniversary. They killed an ox & had a lovely station (12:30) dinner. I made "toffee" & fudge & sent to them. Baths – mended, etc. (Back ache.)

June 14 – Sorted clothes in 4 trunks until 11 a.m. Fried steak & helped with cooking dinner. Made date cake for Feterary Tessima & one for us. (Went to 6 p.m. rest so tired I could hardly get to bed.) Daddy dear & John went to town to see about Gamo iron. Then Hal went to F. Tessima's with bread & cake. Too tired to sleep or rest well all night & my darling didn't ever go to sleep all night.

June 16 – My darling's glasses came, Praise the Lord (by carrier) Letter from Speedy's ($30 M. T. check) U.S. mail – Allen's $7 U.S. & Ethel tells of $40 in transmission to us. Our God knows our need & praise His name, His smile of approval is sweet. Made cookies for Gamo & Mr. Lewis going next Mon. Baths – Sunday preparation – wash my hair, etc.

June 20 – (Bath day) aches & pains continue.

June 21 – Thursday. Slept from 10 to 12:30 only – pains becoming more severe – sent for Dr. about 7:30 a.m. Our precious Bobby Boy arrived at 12:25 p.m. ["7 lbs." written in margin] God so graciously undertook. How we praise Him!

June 22 – Mrs. Roberts's birthday. The kiddies & Daddy went to her birthday supper. Iraba staying "on duty" with Bobby & me.

June 24 – Quiet Sunday.

July 1 – Got up & walked around in bedroom & living room for a little while today. Feel pretty well for the first, tho "tottery."

July 6 – The most terrible attack yet, my lover had this night suffering most intensely. Balacho, Mrs. R., Lois & I working hard 3 full hrs. trying to bring some relief. He became numb all over – nerves & circulation likely, much atropine & morphine given, but of little avail. For some hours after, he couldn't move even his hand or lift his head. Dr. R[oberts] is in Chincha.

July 7 – My sweetheart is so weak & exhausted. An attack like that (or even a lesser one) can't be gotten over for days. How I wish I could help him in these terrible illnesses.

July 8 – Sun. My darling feels a bit stronger today, but is so weak he must stay in bed – in fact, he is too much exhausted to object.

July 10 – My darling had another attack last night. Not as severe as last Friday night's, but bad enough. Lois & Mrs. Roberts took care of him. (Dr. is still in Shamma, caring for the Bumnas children – pneumonia & ear infections.) (Gudama & Brom's wedding day.)

July 12 – Dr. R. returned yesterday.

July 13 – Another gall stone attack last night. It was a severe one, but did not last as long as that terrible one a week ago tonight. My lover had to stay in bed today however. Oh how he suffers & my heart goes out to him.

July 14 – Mr. Lewis came back from Gamo. One carrier died at Azoh en route, due to exposure & exhaustion, on the return trip.

July 15 – What a precious, happy Sunday our little family spent together realizing this would be our last Sunday for many weeks we could be together; therefore asked God to make this day especially precious & He did.

July 16 – Our first sunny day. Dr. & Mrs. Lewis & my darling conferred about the A.A. trip this forenoon deciding it would be taken next

Thurs. I mended my sweetheart's clothes and began preparations for his going. John Truwin is to accompany him to Lambuda. Mr. Cowser from there to Maraka & some one from Akaki come out there to meet him & go to A.A. with him.

July 17 – We prayed for good weather in order to dry the washing if it was God's will & the sun shone the entire day. Consequently everybody's colds are clearing up from the sunshine. My lover took a boy & bought a field of hay this p.m.

July 18 – Carriers in – letters & allowances came, thank God. All morning my lover & I got food, supplies, etc. together, in the p.m. sewed bags, packed, etc., getting to bed about 11 p.m. Oh, if only I could go with him to be near in his time of need! Surely this is a supreme test, but God will not suffer us to be tempted above what we are able to bear, etc.

July 19 – My own darling left this morning for Addis Ababa & Gulaly – oh, how my heart aches! God only knows the suffering of a soul, but <u>He</u> <u>does</u> <u>know</u> & His comfort is precious. Unto Him we've committed ourselves, our all & He faileth never. His grace is sufficient. I know whom I have believed & He doth all things well.

July 20 – Wrote to Mrs. Wright, Mrs. Barton, Hoopers & my lover last nite & to Mrs. Lambie (thanking her for the grapefruit) this a.m. & sent it back by the carrier. Roberts & Lois came over for about ¾ hr. last eve. to help cheer me up. We had supper tonight with them. How I miss my darling! Wrote to him & Kathrine, then fed Bobby at 10:30 p.m.

July 21 – Bobby Dear is one month old today. My sweetheart reached Lambuda this p.m. (4 o'clock). What days! What sorrow! How I have to keep looking to Him Who alone knows the grief of my heart!

July 22 – Tried to be cheerful and to make the day pleasant for the kiddies. (Sunday.)

July 23 – My thots are always with my lover! I spend all my mornings with schoolwork, caring for Bobby & Junior at the same time. Duronie letter from my darling. Praise the Lord.

July 24 – Very bad electrical storm from 9 to 10:30 p.m. Junior was so frightened. My days are so full, but not any more so than my mind & heart with thots of & love for my darling. I can hardly think of my work or keep my thots "gathered together" to write letters or do anything else than that which I must do such as caring for these sweet, dear God-given kiddies.

July 25 – A carrier brot letters. (Wrote to my darling in evening.) Phone message from Sidamo called Dr. over there so he left this p.m. I wonder where my darling is tonight. He's surrounded by His love & care, I know, & I'm continually looking to Him to meet our every need. Somehow I'm looking to Him to bring praise to His name thru this all.

July 26 – A whole week (it seems ages more) since my darling rode away on Rhoada. Last nite, our loving Father so graciously sent peace & <u>hope</u> & I believe He is going to give our Daddy back to us again. Oh how good it is to <u>know</u> Him & trust Him for this.

July 27 – Prayer Day – no mention of it here so far as I know, but I am constantly praying anyway these days.

July 29 – Sunday. I wonder if my sweetheart is in Marakko today. (Later – yes, he was, having reached there on Thurs – Friday was prayer day. Sent Negadies off on Sat., while he & Mr. Barton left on Mon.)

July 30 – John T. returned about tea time bringing a precious letter from my darling written last Mon. a.m. just before leaving Lambuda. How glad I was to get it!

August 1 – Miriam's eighth birthday so I told her she might go over & invite Messrs. Lewis, Truwin & Johannus over for lunch. Made a cake. In evening Mrs. R. had a station birthday supper for her & another cake, much to her pleasure. Dr. got in at 5 p.m. Rokes are enroute – in tomorrow. Carried Mrs. Roberts & 4 carriers deserted.

August 2 – It was nearly 6 p.m. by the time the Rokes reached here. Mr. L. had taken carriers out to bring them in. My lover has been gone 2 weeks – oh how much <u>longer</u> it seems.

August 3 – I could hardly sleep last night & all day today a tremendous burden of prayer has stayed on me. God knows the need. Perhaps my darling especially needs prayer just now. God is faithful.

August 4 – Oh praise the Lord – at noon a telegram came stating my own darling one was operated on yesterday & all is well & he's doing well. The relief is great for the strain has been intense. Praise God for undertaking so preciously in our behalf for him! Carrier brought Hal's Marakka letter.

August 5 – (Sent telegram to my darling at Addis.) Sunday, but every day is filled nearly the same, loving & caring for the dear little ones God has so sweetly placed in our care. Went over to see Mrs. Roke & family about 1 hr. in p.m. Oh, how I praise God for letting me know my precious lover is improving. May he soon recover!

August 6 – Called Dr. over. Junior had a temp of 99.6. Dr. gave needle of Emetine & opened both ear drums. They are draining. How glad I am to know Hal is better on top of this. <u>He</u> keeps reminding me, "He stayeth His east wind in the day of His north wind." Jr. slept or cried practically all day – slept fairly well at nite.

August 7 – Lillie & Laurie got in at supper-time, unexpectedly. Junior is seemingly better. All have colds. Boys washed.

August 8 – Junior seems better – ear still draining. Kept Miriam in bed nearly all day trying to get her over her cold. We all have grip, except Bobby. He's fine. Lilly came over at noon. Bocula on duty this morning having had dysentery since last week & not working at all this wk.

August 9 – 3 wks. ago my lover left. Miriam & Paul in bed – fear pneumonia for Miriam. Little sleep for me these nites.

August 10 – A wk ago today, God gave "skillfulness of hands." Praise His name & my darling continues to improve, I trust. Miriam's better – Paul still in bed trying to keep him from getting worse. My cold is a bit better.

August 11 – Mrs. Roke's & Mr. Lewis' birthdays. Dr. had to re-open Junior's left ear about 8 p.m. Miriam is improving. Bobby was sick all day, due to my onions, I fear – cried almost all the time from about 4 a.m. until early Sun. a.m.

August 12 – Sunday & the kiddies prayed tonite – thanking God for this "good Sunday." Yes, He knows & has strengthened 'tho I hardly closed my eyes all nite due to Bobby's colic. The poor dear has slept nearly all day, being completely worn out. Mail came – Miriam's birthday letter included from Ethel – also Ed's letter.

August 13 – Bobby still sleeps mostly, but his stomach is better, – took 1½ ozs. milk – the most since Friday's illness. Sent Ed's check by gov't post to my lover today. Bobby became very ill about noon. Dr. opened both ears – temp 102° – at 11:30 p.m. temp 104.2. I sat & held him most all night – by a.m., better. Opened one of M's ears also – left channel too irregular & small to open.

August 14 – "As thy days, so shall thy strength be." Harry Markham's birthday. Bobby frightened me terribly at noon, – I thought he might be "going." Tonite, he's _much_ better praise the Lord. Miriam & Junior are improving, too. Bobby took 1½ oz. milk at 8 p.m. – took 1½ hrs. to get it down, but it was worth the time. Mrs. Roke & Lillie are improving. I trust my lover is.

August 15 – Baths – continued nursing of all the dear kiddies. (entered 8/19)

August 17 – Mail (gov't.) from Margaret Gourley (£3+). Paxton ladies (£6+) through Ethel Johnson, machine needles, Zan, A. Aden's, & Moore's. Carrier enroute who, I do trust, is bringing the most desired mail of all – a letter from my darling. Thank God, tho for this much needed money. Wrote to Zan, Kathrine & Mrs. A. – Goffa & my lover.

August 18 – Baths – kiddies improving – Paul in bed all day today – still painting all our throats, washing Bobby's ears, etc. Started a letter to Gourleys. Carrier not in yet. Weather & roads too bad for him to get thru in usual time. Lillie is up – Mrs. Roke improving.

August 19 – Sunday. My darling has been gone a month. Oh that it were 3 – then he'd soon be with us again, if not by now! Junior has 1° fever today – others normal. Paul has a sty coming & has to keep bathing it with hot (boric acid) water which eases it. I'm tired, but trusting! Carriers came about 7 p.m., bringing Dr. L.'s letter & things from my darling. So glad he is improving.

August 20 – Snatched every minute possible to write letters.

August 21 – Bobby is 2 mo. old. Carrier left with two Paxton drafts for Hal. Kiddies still have some sickness, but are improving.

August 22 – <u>Tired</u> tonight. Baths – got half the mats down in the bedroom. Taking Miriam's temp. every 3 hrs. – very irregular – from normal to 1° extra different time during the day – Baffling!

August 23 – Miriam's temp thus – 99.1, 100°, 99.6, 99.2. Dr. is trying medicine for rheumatic fever. Paul's eyes are well. Junior is memorizing Scrip. vs., poems, counting, the scale, etc. So fast these days. He is rapidly developing. Bobby's ears draining <u>very</u> much. He seems normal otherwise. I wrote to my lover this afternoon.

August 24 – So glad for mail about my darling. Dr. L. & nurse Templeton both wrote. How very sick he has been. God bless & meet him. Dr. R. says Miriam does have rheumatic fever – white blood count is 11000, it should be 6000+. He examined me – not to pleased. On my feet too much – uterus tipped & too big, etc., etc.

August 25 – Wrote to Aunt Clara, my lover, & Ethel Johnson & Paxton group to be mailed tomorrow morning. The sun shone more today than for many weeks – so cheering. Bobby's ears still draining "lots."

August 26 – Sunday.

August 28 – So tired tonite! A carrier came bringing my precious lover's letter – his first & oh how welcome! My whole being cries out with & for him. God bless him & meet his <u>every</u> need. I want to write to him <u>so</u> much, but I'm so tired & exhausted I just can't think or write.

August 29 – Wrote to Hoopers, Miss Templeton & my darling so the carrier can take them early tomorrow a.m. Miriam is still in bed running a slight fever. Bobby's ears still draining a great deal. Sun has shone most of each day since Sun. What a blessing & relief from the fog & cold of <u>weeks</u>.

September 8 – Precious letter from my darling – his second since his operation. Other good mail.

September 9 – Bobby's ears stopped draining.

September 10 – Dr. R. quite concerned over my "innards."

September 12 – Made 2 batches of fudge (1st went to sugar so kept it here) so I could send some to my lover with Lillie for our wedding anniversary.

September 13 – Lillie & Laurie left this a.m. for A.A. for her gall bladder operation. Miriam still runs a temp.

September 22 – Miriam sat in big deck chair in the sun an hour today & enjoyed it greatly. She ate her supper with a relish tonite, the first time for many weeks. How happy she was to have on her clothes. How glad we all are to be better & to know my lover is, too. Wrote to him.

September 23 – Sunday. Anderson's ate dinner here. Zillah kindly stayed with the kiddies, & I went to the evening communion service at Roberts' – sweet time – better spirit. How I long for my lover!

September 24 – Pulled 4 (or parts of 4) of Miriam's teeth – took 1 hr all told. She must stay in bed now <u>all</u> the time. Special prayer day. Zillah stayed here so I could go in aft. – a real prayer spirit was there. Mr. Anderson's birthday so cake & tea followed.

September 25 – Miriam feels good today, but has an extra degree of temp.

September 26 – Praise the Lord! A great shout went up when my own precious lover got in today at noon surprising me for our 10th wedding anniversary tomorrow. How <u>thin</u> he is, but thank God, he is here & nearly well.

Hal on Pax—9/27/34 at Soddo. "Pax was purchased with a gift from Paxton friends, consequently the name. Taken at Soddo just after Hal's return from Addis Ababa after his operation."

September 27 – 10 years of blessed joy together – my darling husband & I. Roberts had wedding cake (orange blossoms 'n all) for us. Phillips, Andersons, Lois, Messrs. Lewis & John, etc. being there – nice time. Zillah insisted on staying with our kiddies so we could go. The Lord is good to us. (Miss Reilly fell from horse enroute.)

September 29 – Bobby is lovely.

September 30 – Sunday. How sweet to have my darling here – the first Sunday for <u>such</u> a <u>long</u> time.

Home in Soddo, 1934

October 3 – Paul is 7 today. Had Messrs. Lewis, Truwin, and Johannus for his birthday dinner. Had fresh strawberries & cake for dessert.

October 6 – … Dr. sent me home to bed for 2 weeks. … My lover is busy buying gulalie mules.

October 7 – In bed all day. Feels good to rest & read. Feeding Bobby in bed to help a bit.

October 14 – Sunday – Soddo – Kenneth Anderson was born today – hard time for his mother – "Caesarean"

October 29 – Monday. Beginning today with 15 minutes out-of-doors, Dr. is trying Miriam with the sun to see if that will help build her up. My precious one & I are busy preparing for his going to Gamo next Thursday, DV [Lord willing]. Paul is going, too. He is thrilled!!

November 1 – Up to now, 157 days my lover has had to be away. My darlings, (Daddy & Paul) left just after noon for Gamo, taking Pru, too. How empty the house seems without them! They hope to finish the house enough for us to go down very soon, D.V. as soon as Miriam is able. She's been out in the sun awhile each day this week & is having a nearly normal temp.

November 2 – Peg's birthday so Mrs. Roberts had 4 p.m. tea in her honor. How empty our house continues! 1 letter from Paul & Ruth Carlson only.

November 4 – Sunday. Peg & John came over during the forenoon. Had a quiet day with S.S. [Sunday School] for M. & Jr. in the afternoon.

November 5 – Working hard on Paul's coveralls in afternoon & until quite late at night (11 p.m.)

November 6 – Good letter from my lover this p.m. Miriam's temp. has been normal for a week – praise the Lord. Sewed more on Paul's coveralls. Wrote 3 letters.

November 7 – Bobby has had diarrhea for over a week so I gave him C. oil today & a formula of half milk & water. Finished the coveralls & made cookies to send to my lover.

November 8 – Bobby seems to be improving. He keeps playing happily and acts well. Made preserves for Gamo. Mail of no consequence today, so John won't send Gamo post mail until later.

November 9 – Bobby really is better & has slept much of today. Spent 2 hrs. on lang. this aft. & eve. The Lord will provide proven – down to 3 T's for two days & 5 Thalers came. (Peg & John were the instruments & Miriam.)

November 11 – Sunday spent quietly with Miriam & Junior telling Bible stories.

November 15 – What a wonderful answer to prayer today's mail proved to be! God is faithful, & we praise Him for all.

November 17 – at 2:10 a.m. Henry Phillips arrived. Peg & he are doing well. Finished preparing & packing the things to send Tiginia to Gamo so he left just after noon to go to my lover. (send funds) Busy getting mail ready for A.A. carriers to take back with them tomorrow.

November 18 – Sunday. Sent off carriers – also order for Miriam's sweater with $5.00 U.S. to pay for same, etc. to Lillie.

November 20 – Praise the Lord! Miriam is <u>up</u> today, the first since Aug. 7th. Dr. circumcised Bobby this p.m. I'm longing for my lover.

November 21 – Made mincemeat (1 qt.) for Thanksg[iving]. 2 huge wonderful boxes from A. Minnie – just what we need so I'm sure the Lord guided her.

November 22 – Bobby is getting along well as is Miriam also. Tiginia hasn't yet come at 2 p.m. so no mail from my lover. Made apple & peach butter for us and Anderson's.

November 23 – My darling Lover & Paul got home, announced to me by Pru, this a.m. How pleased I am! The Lord is good.

November 29 – Thanksgiving Day, spent packing & getting ready to leave. Had a nice time together, nevertheless, as a little family.

December 3 – Monday 8:30 a.m. Left Soddu for Gamo.

December 4 – Spent p.m. at Baroda entertaining "big" men & was just ready to retire when the "big" woman was announced. Tired!

December 5 – At Azō in p.m. with entertaining again all p.m. Big men very friendly – one gave us a sheep.

December 6 – <u>Home</u> in Gamo, praise God! Nick had a wonderful dinner prepared, & it is <u>so</u> good to get here. We've had a good trip.

December 7 – Working to get in order a bit for the Roberts' & Lois coming as well as for our convenience.

December 8 – Getting baking etc. done for Nick's & Mal's going next Monday.

December 9 – Roberts' & Lois spent the day here. Had an afternoon service with Nick speaking, Hal leading.

December 10 – Nick left before sunrise & Mal went just after lunch.

December 25 – Xtmas, truly a day of thanks because the Son of God has come, praise His name! Just our own little family here, but happy indeed to be together with Him as our Joy & Portion. Little things were gathered together for the kiddies, plus a dear pkg. from Zan & Peg made it pleasant for them & we, Hal & I, don't have our hearts set on these things, anyway.

December 31 – Rhoada left today for Soddo to bring Miss Bray here eventually. Sent ground cherries to Roberts who'd sent 3½ doz. eggs to me.

Chapter 4

1935, Soddo and Gamo

January 1 – The same as any other day in Ethiopia. We almost forgot to wish each other happy new year, but desire it to be our best for the Lord Jesus Christ, should He tarry. Happy to be here & well.

January 3 – Negadis came with mats & mail – 5 P.M. Wrote to Sara & Arthur A. & Sarah & Roy Wright.

January 4 – Negadis left, also Iraba, for Soddu, taking our mail & ground cherries to R's, also fly for Miss Bray's tent. Wrote to Betty Stauffer, Chenaults.

January 18 – Bobby has a fever with vomitting.

January 19 – Balacho & Cossah went to Timcot celebrations. Bailey people calling God because of the "sick moon" (eclipse) at 7 p.m. [pagan worship]

January 20 – "Timcut." Bobby's fever left this p.m. – a little rash seems to be appearing on him. Had a pleasant Sun. Supper on porch 1st time. Natives here all a.m. Rest [for Miriam important] in p.m., etc.

January 23 – Bobby's throat must not be quite as sore. He took his food much better & in larger quantities. Rash is somewhat "watery."

January 27 – Sunday. Miriam & my lover went to Fitawrari Sailies. Tiginia came at 4:30 (26 letters plus magazines).

January 29 – Baked etc, plus regular duties. Grandmother is 84. Rain (little 10 min. shower) just after we retired.

January 30 – We had a precious birthday. How good the Lord is to have given me my darling & dear little Junior, too. More rain (little) about 8:30 p.m.

January 31 – My lover didn't eat much supper. He felt too weary & his head ached. Perhaps, too much sun. Children's school 3 hrs. Language 1 hr. Others all well.

February 3 – Sunday. "Pru" died this a.m.

February 4 – All a.m., my lover had a bad headache & nausea followed in the p.m. by a severe attack of appendicitis, presumably. Thank God for deliverance finally.

February 5 – My lover weak & tired, but much improved for which we praise God.

February 6 – All has gone well this busy day.

February 9 – Another slighter attack for my sweetheart, but "God is able" & our trust is in Him.

February 10 – Sun. My darling arose late & was weary all day so rested much.

February 16 – Bobby has a bad diarrhea. Gave castor oil to him. (Began yesterday.) Junior is cross.

February 17 – Junior is "spotted" with some illness & seems to have a slight fever. Bobby is better, but we felt it was best to give chlorodyne. Miss Bray's 1st carriers came.

February 21 – Miss Bray arrived around 3 – 3:30 P.M. from Baroda. Much rain during night & occasional showers today. I'm weary!

February 24 – My sweetheart awakened this a.m. with an attack which continued until after we retired at 10:30 p.m.

February 25 – I spent the day in bed – weary! – Aunt Maude's birthday (50). My darling went to see Dejaz. Bunna at his request. Merely wants a photo taken of his church next Thurs.

February 26 – Bobby's first tooth was seen today. He has dysentery, I think. Gave chlorodyne. Hal still has pain today, but insists on working on a birthday gift for me – the lover!

February 27 – Had a delightful birthday because my loving Father permitted our little family to be together. Miss Bray came over here & made a birthday [cake]. Then, at my invitation, stayed to enjoy it with us.

March 10 – 4 carriers & postmen came calling Hal to Soddu to perform the double wedding ceremony next Thurs. for Cowsers & Forsbergs. Miss Bray led eve. meeting.

March 11 – Got off carriers & things in order for Hal's leaving early in the a.m. Bobby is well. Miriam has cold.

March 12 – My lover left soon after five for Soddo.

March 14 – Weddings for Cowsers and Forsbergs. Tiny shower tonite!

March 15 – Little shower about 8 P.M.

March 16 – Gudana came at supper-time bringing the mail & my sweetheart's good letter. Miriam still has a cold – others well. Little rain & much wind at 8:30 P.M. Dr. suspects bad appendix.

March 17 – Quiet Sunday. Wrote to McCrearys, Showers, Katherine & Rachael jointly. Miss Bray & I had a little eve. service. (Negadies with groceries at 7 P.M. in the wind storm.)

March 18 – Walamo carriers came about 7 to 9 P.M. Letter from my lover.

March 19 – Wrote to my darling & sent it to him via the carriers who were returning to Soddu. (He received it at Baroda.)

March 20 – My own Darling & Mr. Devers arrived from Soddu. Pax was left at Baroda with Balacho. How good to have my lover again!

March 21 – Bobby is 9 mo. today. I've been "dragging around" for days – don't know why!

March 22 – Miss Bray, Mr. Devers & Hal went to see the Dejazmatch at his summons. I had school, looked after house, cooked, etc., all day.

March 23 – Junior had to have silver nitrate put into his right eye.

March 24 – Junior had "silver" in both eyes. Dejazmatch Tiginia & a friend of Gudana's to entertain a.m. 2 services in a.m.

April 3 – Bobby has conjunctivitis. Junior's eyes are weak, but well. Thank God!

April 18 – Hal is making a cupboard for Paul's & Junior's room; Tom D, a bathroom door. Miss Bray is mending our trek bed. I washed several best dresses. My tooth & face continues aching. Bobby's eyes are much improved!

April 19 – Aunt Minnie is 52 today. Seems impossible.

April 21 – Easter – "The Lord is risen!"

April 29 – Forsbergs left for Goffa. Hal & I busy packing to leave for Soddu in A.M.

April 30 – Negadis refused (Tessima) so couldn't leave. "All things" since my lover had a bad attack last nite. Rained all forenoon.

May 1 – After tumbling down the hill as a result of the Blumbera's mules [heals] & fear, I started on Fip. The mule ran away soon after, breaking the girth so my lover had to go back, not catching up for some hours (& incidentally not getting wet). We reached Azo at 4 P.M. God bless the kiddies. Rained just as tent was set up.

May 2 – Left camp early, reaching Baroda at 12:30 – more rain just after the tent was up. Stopt to see the Priest friends the next day.

May 3 – On to Gulcha, left at 7 a.m. Stopt at "big" woman's & priest's, leaving again at 2 p.m. after a shower. We soaked 3 times in drenching African rains which took us 2 days to dry out from. Reached Gulcha at 2:30 p.m., tired.

May 4 – Alarm at 4:00 a.m. Boys were slow so didn't get away much earlier than other days. Reached Soddu at 11:30 a.m. relieving their minds as they looked for us Thurs. & Fri. Dr. examined Hal Sunday.

May 5 – Sunday. How our prayers & thots are with those darlings the Lord has given us! Dr. & Lois removed the nail on the sore finger.

May 6 – My lover has had nausea & pain, really a minor attack today & his finger hurts. I wrote to Adamson's.

May 7 – My lover's attack has made him so weary & nauseated he has had to remain all day in bed on a liquid (no lunch). He feels better this evening. At 3 P.M. John Phillips & Mr. Mitchell arrived. Carrier in – no allowances, none since Jan. which was the last for '34. Wrote to "B.D," Miss Templeton.

May 8 – Wrote to Rachael & Kath. jointly & Mrs. H. W. Hester – also Miss Templeton & Fern and Bob Burns. My lover feels better.

May 13 – Dr. said today to plan on the operation Wed. morning. The "peace of God" & "the God of peace" is our portion!

May 14 – My darling is to be prepared tonite for his appendectomy tomorrow. Truly the Lord <u>is</u> a very present help in time of need & our eyes are unto Him who fails not.

May 15 – (Wed.) At 5 to 9 this a.m., Dr. gave the "hypo" followed by the anesthetic for my <u>precious</u> one. It wasn't easy for me, but God sweetly sustained. At 9:30 the <u>light</u> went on & continued until exactly 11:45. The appendix was much enlarged, adhered & bad. How glad we are it is "out." My lover wasn't much nauseated & didn't wholly come out of the ether until 7:00 P.M. A hypo soon followed so he wouldn't feel the pain. I slept <u>very</u> little.

May 16 – My darling is very weary & having many gas pains. A rising temp (to 103°) indicates something was wrong. At 10:30 Lois called Roberts & the three worked until 2 a.m. re-opening & soaking the infected finger. I slept better, but am still tired & sleepy – due to the strain. Negadis disturbing previous night, etc. Peg, John & Bunny returned to Duronsie today.

May 17 – My sweetheart is very tired after his strenuous, painful night, but he has no extra temp. Kept hot applications & water bottles on his arm nearly 5 hrs., apparently afraid of blood poisoning (?!). It was blood poisoning. He is much improved, tho uncomfortable due to gas pains, etc. tonight. Sent Cossa to Gamo. Bassa is peeved over something. Dr. [disciplined] him, I learned later so hope that proves effective, D.V.

May 18 – My darling is doing better today. How glad I am and thankful!

May 19 – My lover is doing very well this eve. We had a precious time reading Philippians & praying together. Retired at 8 P.M. "Big lady" from Baroda called & a leading man from there sent his servant with greetings and to inquire about my darling. No service tonight. Mrs. Mitchell in a little pain.

May 20 – My sweetheart had a bad night last night due to the poisoning which localized in an abscess in the incision. Dr. [Roberts] opened it about 1 a.m. & consequently, Hal is very tired & in bad pain today.

May 21 – My darling had a better day, praise the Lord. The outer stitches were removed, making him more comfortable. Much rain this week.

May 22 – Rains in "torrents" still. Cossa returned from home. All is well, praise God there. Hal had a good night (last) & a splendid day. Clips removed.

May 23 – I moved to Lewis' today. Mail came late in p.m. $25 from the Lord in Mr. Runyon's letter. How true – sweetly so – "God moves in mysterious ways His wonders to perform."

May 24 – My lover sat up an hour this a.m. & p.m. Had tea (a.m.) & supper out of bed. The Lord is good!

May 25 – My sweetheart was up longer today & is doing well.

May 26 – Sunday. My lover was up a good while today & <u>dressed</u>. Praise God for His goodness to us! Our thoughts go to the dear kiddies much today, but God is there.

May 27 – Hal moved to Lewis' with me today. How good it is to have him back!

May 28 – Busy trying to catch up on letters today.

May 29 – Made two hospital gowns for Lois, had baths, etc. Tiginia arrived. Much trouble & sickness in Gamo. The dear kiddies! God is able & we believe Him.

May 30 – Decoration day [in the States] – forgotten out here. Wrote 3 letters & wash my hair in a.m. Mail from Paxton church & friends with enclosed check of almost £14, Surely "Before they call," etc. proven again. {All applied on our Soddu expenses.}

May 31 – Sent for Xtian science books.

June 1 – At nearly 11 P.M. the Mitchell heir arrived. We had supper at John's. John Edwin Mitchell – 9 lbs.

June 2 – Had breakfast with John, too.

June 3 – Wrote 3 letters. 2 carriers came – still no allowance for 1935 & over 5 mo. have passed. It is well our trust is in <u>God</u>. He is faithful!

June 5 – Good news from Shammah tonight – All is well – praise the Lord. Surely He <u>never</u> fails. Oh, I'm so glad I've been taught by Him to really trust Him, for truly He is worthy, Hallelujah! (Getting <u>so</u> eager to get home again.)

June 8 – Packed our boxes for going home.

June 9 – Sun. Hal gave a dear message on the "Song of Solomon" at Roberts' to the profit of all. Communion following. Late to bed – talk with Ray.

June 10 – [Note in margin] John Roger Anderson arrived. Tired both tonight.

At 10:50, we left for home, Hal on Fip, & I on Hopey. Very good day. Reached camp at about 4 P.M. (Gulcho). The Lord is working. He even had the road "made plain" for us (Bienna's wife).

June 11 – Left about 6:25 getting to Baroda at noon, stopped at two priests' homes. Gifts of eggs, chicken, popped hafra corn, "bacala" etc. "Big Lady" called late in afternoon. Met Bienna's wife near Baroda. Whole caravan stopped to greet us. Tiniest shower at supper time.

June 12 – Left at 6:25 again, reaching Azo thru a fog at nearly noon. Various callers arrived. Hal went to see "Otto Malcah." He later brot us a lamb, ingeria, etc. Killed the lamb, had some for supper, give "boys" the liver & brot the rest home. A good shower about 8 p.m.

June 13 – 6:25 a.m. left, reaching home about 11:30. Oh how good it is to see the dear children & to find them all looking so well. (tho Miriam's eyes still look weak.). They all came way out to meet us, Tom included. At Chincha a shower preceded us & near Shama, we had a "drizzle" only, not requiring raincoats. Truly an answer to prayer during June to not get wet once enroute home!

June 14 – Bobby is getting acquainted with me, today. Yes today, Miss Bray, only, looked good to him. I'm getting into the "harness" by degrees.

June 15 – Did Tom's packing for his going Mon.

June 16 – Sun. A carrier came in about 4 P.M. following up the mail at supper time. Aunt Minnie's pkg. & the one we ordered from Lennard's (blankets, boots, etc.) came. How good our Father is to us so graciously watching over us & "ours"! Jan. allowances & kiddies' 1st quar. came, praise His Name!

June 17 – Sorted various articles to send to others (missionaries). Wrote to Zan. Natives are all so cordial in their greeting & welcoming us. Wood came all day long – hay is coming, too & occasionally some eggs. Beautiful p.m.

June 18 – Another clear, sunshiny day – not like the rainy season. All the clothes got dry by this p.m.

June 20 – School, entertaining Dectah Amhara (Zebh) & wife & a few preparation for tomorrow, etc. Set out calandulahs with M. P. & Jr. as assts. along front walk.

June 21 – And our dear Bobby is one year old! What a darling he is! 20½ pounds of sweetness, vitality, and beauty! Miss Bray invited for dinner. The kiddies all had a happy day.

June 24 – Bassa left our services tonite. He doesn't like this fog & damp weather.

June 30 – Sun. Miss Bray led in p.m. service. Tiginia arrived, but no mail, to speak of. The 2nd half of June, pretty fair weather for rainy season, but foggier lately.

July 1 – Gubaro "entered" as an "ashcar." He seems quick, willing & pleasant.

July 4 – Kiddies made American flags in school. Hal had native school as usual in the p.m. Miss Bray came over & shared our pancake supper. Heavy fog continues these days, but about ½ hr. of sun around 5 p.m.

July 14 – Sun. Bocula of Chincha came today, as usual lately on Sundays. Glad we are for the guchas of eggs he brings! How lovely, greatly appreciated sun. Very little mail. I spoke on our riches in Christ (abundance in Script.) Earthly v. Heavenly Riches.

July 17 – Oh how our loving Father has undertaken for us during this past year. Two operations & opportunities to prove Him!

July 19 – My lover left for A.A. Hallelujah! What a Savior!

July 20 – Bocula, wife, mother & sister of Chincha, came at 11:30, in need of "murphies," delaying Miss Bray's & my [trip] to Gulta until 1:30 p.m. Fetuarie Sailie was having court on the mt. side above the river, which he left to greet us. Had a delightful 1½ hrs. at their home – learned to play 1 tune on an "instrument of <u>10</u> strings." Home at 6 p.m. Foggy!

July 21 – Tiny bit of sun today. There has been more sunny days this past week, with little rain than for a long time. Thank the Lord for His keeping us in health these days! No money since Feb. has come to us from mission other than the <u>small</u> Jan. allowance, which was kept in A.A. in our B.A. (in June.) The Lord is our Provider, however & He never has & never will fail.

July 23 – Praise God from whom all blessings flow! Negadis arrived with the long-delayed <u>April</u> order. How glad we are for the supplies. Ed Cording & Ruth James' wedding day.

July 25 – Special carrier – news: <u>All U.S. citizens ordered by the U.S. Gov't. to evacuate immediately via Kenya.</u> Mission: <u>Act freely accdg to the Lord's leading</u>. Junior's & Miriam's shoes came. Thank the Lord!

July 26 – How good it is to have something other than Paul's old shoes on Junior or a pr. of bedroom slippers! Hal still has to wear his boots, however as those that came from England didn't fit so had to be returned.

July 28 – A good Sun. My lover brot another dear message on the Song of Solomon.

July 31 – Called on Bocula's "mother." He is in chains. Baked Miriam's birthday cake & made her a slip, plus other duties.

August 1 – Miriam is 9. – had a happy day.

August 2 – Went to a weeping – baby boy, only child, dead. Gave out the Word, thru Balacho, as did Miss Bray, very earnestly.

August 3 – Chincha Amhara & wife, called. Miss B & I went to visit Buldena-Muldue wife & newborn baby boy. (2 other children before – both dead.) **Aselīfech** interpreted (unsatisfactorily) the Word of God. Visited Bocula's mother too.

August 4 – Been preparing message on I Cor. 13 for tonite. My lover & I have had delightful peace over war trouble.

August 5 – Mail arrived in evening. The Lord is good to us, praise His name! Much company all day today, includ'g Chincha "silk soh" for vaccine. None here.

August 6 – Feterarie Sailies' "mist" sent for hair dye from me today via Cassah whom Miss Bray sent there on an errand. (She wants to sell her things so told them.)

August 7 – My lover & Balacho went visiting in nearby huts, getting home at noon – raining. People busy getting "gubs" planted. I made Robert's food & had school all a.m.

August 11 – Bobby began to walk a few steps alone several times today. He <u>prefers</u> to hold on to one finger of someone, however.

August 13 – Monday, ugly day no clothes dried.

August 14 – Tues. beautiful day, warm and sunny. Paul has a "buggy" top which I keroseened & hope I've kill them all.

August 15 – Gudana & Ginjah arrived bringing mail, the former to tell God's Word to the Gamos! May they listen & many accept Him. Ohman's coming early in Oct. We'll enjoy them.

August 16 – Balacho went to Chincha, [L]idge Johanas' etc, attempting to cash our allowance check, but no one would. "Auchawcheet" still "on" there due to [murder] (shot) of the Negadras.

August 17 – Keroseening Paul today – apparently I didn't get them all the first time. Cassah did the same thing for the black calf. Nearly all week has been beautiful, warm, weather.

August 18 – Hal & I went visiting several neighbors in p.m. Mail arrived after supper. Hal spoke on Paul's "3–I am readys."

August 19 – Sara & Art sent 13.46 M.T. so that, plus $1 U.S. to Miriam from Mrs. Lewis & $2 to us from friends (Dalbey & Adens) pd. Miss Bray in full to date. Wrote letters all day.

August 22 – Gudana left, planning to return after Muskol. Aunt Ella died—"stroke."

August 23 – Miss Bray & I travelled [Dieta] – ward landing at Tungah's mother's home finally. He has a new brother – (Hagar-method). Gave out the gospel in a few huts. "Why tell us," say the women. "Tell the men first!"

August 24 – "Sue" [the dog] came today & the kiddies are thrilled! She seems to like us.

August 25 – Sun. Bobby has a cold. Psa. 87:7, "All my springs are in thee," my subject for tonight's service. God gave liberty & blessing.

August 26 – My lover, Cassah & Ahlumoh went to Sharrah, being gone from 7 A.M. to 6 P.M., returning tired, & riding Pax from Fiterari Sailie's.

August 27 – Planned to go to Chincha with Miss B. to visit Bocula's "mother" who is ill, but day too dark & damp (as has been all week so we didn't go – Sat. /31).

August 29 – Sharrah Shum came to return Hal's visit bringing us a gusha of 68 ears of corn.

August 30 – Had a sweet day of prayer, the Lord being in our midst.

August 31 – Bobby & Junior's colds (of a week's duration) seem better today after using drops of argarol last night & today.

September 1 – Due to Miss Bray's cold, I took the service – "The Life that pleases God." Tiginia arrived just after, Bergland's fine pkge, many letters (all concerned over war news & wondering if we're enroute to the U.S.A.). Dad seeking [divorce] news, Eileen's terrible experience, etc, etc. To sleep at 1 a.m., bad headache & upset stomach due to eye strain, I fear.

September 2 – Labor Day!

September 4 – Miss B. & I went to Chincha to give "memphies" [messages] getting home at 6 P.M. Rained hard – "soaked," cold, tired.

Fip & I slipped repeatedly – "All things to all men, that might win some." So good to get home to all.

September 5 – Apparently I didn't take cold, but carrying around aches from riding & slipping in the mud.

September 12 – Mats from Soddo arrived in a downpour. We need them <u>so</u> much. Raspberries, Calla lilies, Irises, & Geraniums also. – no mail.

September 13 – Got living room mats down, etc. Mending every p.m. trying to get caught up. Bobby walks alone pretty well now. Very heavy rains all this week & fog!

September 22 – At sunset, Bahone and Tora came bringing mail & our mule, Praise the Lord for him! Hal spent day in Chincha, tomorrow all Amharas go.

September 27 – Our eleventh milestone [anniversary] of supreme earthly joy! A quiet day. Miss Bray had dinner & supper here. Still busy preparing for our coming guests.

September 29 – Sunday. Mail came. Dear little Graham has gone to be with the Lord "which is <u>far</u> better." Poor, dear Zan and Reg!

September 30 – Killed our big ox. All preparations ready practically for our visitors tomorrow.

October 1 – In a downpour, Ohmans & Ray Davis arrived, Hal accompanying. How glad we are to have them! May their visit be mutually blessed.

October 2 – Hal, Ray, Mr. O & Paul returned from Bailey "sopping wet" in a drenching rain. Tired out & ready to Eat!

1935, Soddo and Gamo

Mabel with Miriam, Paul, Junior, Bobby in carrier behind Mabel—1935

October 3 – Hal made Paul an aeroplane & Ray, a kite so his 8th birthday was pleasant – (gifts from all). Played Pit in evening.

October 4 – Mr. O. and Hal went to Ochola, getting home around 6 P.M. Weary! Supper at Cassah's, then a communion service here after.

October 5 – Shama Negadie refuses to go. Miss Bray, Ray [Davis] & Ohmans left the middle of the A.M. Too bad! We are sorry to see them go. (Made 5 qts mincemeat.)

October 6 – Spent a quiet Sunday alone with our little family & our Lord.

October 7 – Big washing; all dry tho. Rain in evening – much rain last week & all of this (as the following days proved).

October 8 – Spending much time with the kiddies' school all this week, trying to "catch up" a bit. They've done well. Calf today (yellow).

October 9 – School all day. (Threw water all over [Guberoh] – sad!) Hal started "boys" again today. Dumb after vacation!!?!

October 10 – Black calf arrived today. School all day today. Wrote to Margaret Boss. Grandfather Ellis' birthday.

October 13 – Other red cow's calf arrived this a.m. Mail day! Rather small mail.

October 17 – I'm catching cold, I fear.

October 19 – Miriam & I very bad colds – in bed all day. Still it rains! This month has had nothing but torrential rains.

October 20 – Sun. Hal & Paul in bed much of today. (I'd like to be.) <u>All</u> our symptoms like colds are <u>very</u> ugly.

October 21 – Washing failed to dry. Too much rain.

October 22 – Praise the Lord – the sun shone today.

October 23 – Sun. – no rain.

October 25 – My lover spent the day in Chincha, getting home after dark.

October 27 – Sun. Quiet & blessed. Good mail! J.T. & Miss Bray are coming in a wk. or so. 3 older kiddies & Daddy took a p.m. walk to Shama. Jr. did well & is a bit weary.

October 29 – My lover spent the day over the mt. in Shama. A lamb was given to us – another "by mouth," too. Ha!

October 30 – Hal & 3 older kiddies left at 10 a.m. for Alumos, Bailey. The sun has shone, with no rain for more than a wk. Colds all nearly gone now after 2 wk's duration.

October 31 – <u>Slight</u> rain at 10 p.m.

November 1 – My lover ate no supper, nauseated due to a touch of the sun, causing a very bad headache. Let up some about bedtime after rest, aspirin, prayer, etc.

November 2 – Sat. My darling is all right today. Jr. & I have some fresh cold.

November 3 – Sun. Slight showers this forenoon. Cloudy much of the day.

Street family, 1935, Soddo

November 5 – Hard rain last nite, fog today. Ox died, (planned to give it to "boys" for muschol [holiday]). My lover spent this day & nite on road. J.T. & Miss B. & he arrived (11/5) at 10 a.m. Kiddies & I here alone all nite. "God is able."

November 6 – Ill yesterday. John & Miss Bray arrived okay. The Lord met us all, too. Still Jr., B. & I have ugly colds.

November 7 – Rained much of the night & today. Began daily service for the servants & others today in our living room, John speaking.

November 8 – And still it rains! We appreciate both the rain & sun these days in order to get the garden products & flowers well started. (14 natives at a.m. service.)

November 10 – Bobby has a fever & is quite sick – I trust it is only a cold. In bed nearly all day or in Hal's or my arms. Good mail today. John, Hal, Paul & Miriam spent the a.m. calling.

November 11 – Bobby's temp. (under arm) is 99.8° & he feels so sick, feverish, & weak – perspiring which should help.

November 12 – Muschol, big play today. John, Miss Bray & Hal went over to Shamma all day. Bobby is a bit better, tho so weak & sick still. Negadis came, praise the Lord – Jr's. shoes, groc, etc.

November 13 – Spent all a.m. getting Hal & John packed up to go itinerating in Achola. Bobby still sick, but a little better.

November 14 – Bobby choked until stiff & blue – my finger down his throat brot him to the point where he was able again to breathe. I'm wondering if it is whooping cough. Junior put a piece of chalk in his nose, but the Lord delivered & we got it out. What next! Paul sick with intestinal flu, M. in bed with fever & cold, sore throats, Bobby still sick. Yes, "all things," is true & "My grace is sufficient."

November 15 – Bobby coughed much last night. Gave Junior castor oil today. P. M. & I improving, but Junior's throat remains very sore. Let Miriam get up at 9.

November 16 – The middle of the a.m. my lover & John returned. About 1,000 listened at all the services. "hard place, tho." Thurs. my lover was in real pain – indigestion, perhaps. Sat. eve. (today) Bobby is happier than for a wk. Today, Miss Bray asked for her stove – "not now – soon."

November 17 – Sun. Bocula, of Chincha, came this a.m. My lover brought a good message in evening. Tola off – swollen glands – hard cold.

November 18 – Tola still "off." Big weeping nearby. Busy preparing for my darling's Doko trip! Kiddies all improving – how glad we are!

November 19 – The [middle] 8:30 of the morning Hal & John left for Dokko. Made Christmas cake today. (Tola returned this a.m. better!)

November 20 – Oranges, etc came today, Badajoh & father bringing them with one mule. They brot me a letter from my darling & took one to him from me.

November 21 – Made a dark fruit cake for Thanksgiving. Spent the day with kiddies' school.

November 22 – Ditto. Made date bars & batchelor's buttons. Tola off again – sick!

November 23 – John & my lover returned from Dokko. About 400 attended the services there. Tola still off sick so we are "ashcars."

November 24 – Sun. Rain & fog. Garden needs rain. Very little mail came today. 3 baby chicks hatched.

November 25 – My father is 65 today. Tola still sick. Miss Bray gave him a "murphy." 1 more chick today – 2 disappeared.

November 27 – Killed Paul's ox for Thanksgiving. (Bobby vomited once today)

November 28 – Praise ye the Lord – Hallelujah! I brought a message on "Dwell deep" from Jer. 49 [verses] 8 & 30. (Bobby vomited 3 times last night and twice today. May God undertake again!) What a blessed Thanksgiving! Hal & John went to Bailey.

November 29 – Bobby slept well & long last night, so while weak, he is improving. Prayer Day today.

December 1 – Sun. John spoke in evening.

December 3 – Hal & John went over the Shamo mt. today to preach, but thru a misunderstanding as to time, there was no meeting. My darling is very weary these days.

December 4 – Miss Bray & John left for Chincha to do medical work & preach, planning to return Sat. My sweetheart, at noon, couldn't stay up any longer so went to bed. Pains in chest, heart, head, etc. "God is able!"

December 5 – Hal got up today, but had to go back to bed, being too tired to finish breakfast. He felt better later on & spent some time looking after buying hay, etc. Rained!

December 6 – One year in Gamo. We've endeavored to live as unto the Lord & we look to Him to own the year. My lover is better today. Tola still "off."

December 8 – Sunday. Went over to cow chuldies with Hal. Had meeting (Dusita speaking). God is good – shoes came for Hal, Paul & Bobby. Miriam gets Paul's as they are too small. My lover had our evening service. J.T. is sick with a cold. Hal has a stiff neck.

December 10 – J.T. still sick so couldn't go itinerating this week.

December 15 – Very slight mail today.

December 16 – J.T.'s negadies arrived – field council news & foreign mail. J.T. & Miss B. are stationed here. Rachel & Harry in the "press" these days. Out of it, may they find <u>Him</u>. Busy packing & preparing for itinerating meetings beyond Chincha.

December 17 – Left for beyond Chincha today to stay 'till Saturday, so my lover is missed.

December 20 – Invited Miss Bray to lunch with the kiddies & I.

December 21 – John & my lover returned about 1 P.M. Devil-worshippers who didn't want the matter at this last place. Poor souls!

December 22 – Sunday. Bocula's wife spent several hrs. here, including eating dinner with us. He failed to show up. Miriam & Miss Bray accompanied John & Hal to "cow chutalies" (Shamo), but they didn't gather for a service. This makes 3 Sundays. The devil holds his own, "but prayer" etc. Small mail (censored) the last before Christmas.

December 23 – Killed black ox & made preparations for the coming of Fetuarari Gaballis who says he is coming to play & eat tomorrow. Bobby is cutting his first 2 upper molars & hasn't felt too peppy.

December 24 – Bought Miss Bray's stove – $200 M.T.'s. Rained a little. Fetuarari failed to appear. Completed Christmas plans & had a sweet time in eve., singing Christmas songs, etc. after eating Christmas pie, Miss B. prepared here.

December 25 – Had a blessed Christmas. John & Miss Bray spent the day with us. Kiddies so pleased with their stilts, Jr's horse, etc. As usual, Hal & I have each other's love as our gifts, but that is enough.

December 26 – A good soaking rain, lasting 2½ hrs. awakened us, consequently got in many more garden seeds.

December 27 – Prayer day! Rained nearly all night.

December 28 – Rain! John & my darling went to Wōbàràh to make arrangements for itinerating there next week.

December 29 – Sun. In a.m., the three older kiddies & I went visiting at Curka's home. In p.m. "Conchuldie" sent word that he didn't want Hal to come for services as he was going to Chincha for Tamoons. Liar! Paul, Hal & John then went to Deta. Rained last nite.

December 30 – Prepared for "Wobarah" trip. Rained last night, as usual, lately. My darling has a pain like his "old gall bladder pain today. I wonder what it is, but God is able!

December 31 – My lover & John left around 8:30 a.m., returning in a few minutes because of broken "harness." Just as they were again starting the head man of Wobarah arrived to ask them to abide here, not come to his country. Satan!! They went on, promising to stop in Gulta to ask for further permission. What a country!?! Rained again & much fog today. Rained last nite.

Chapter 5

1936, Gamo, Soddo, and War

January 1 – Heavy fog & rain much of the day. Put Miriam to bed because of exhaustion due to heart strain – giving digitalis 3 times a day also. My lover is at Wobarah itinerating. Had school, baths, mended, etc. & hardly remembered this is New Year's. Had Miss B. for lunch. At dark, the mail came – oranges etc. Heard from Ethel – first for 9½ wks. Dr. Hockman dead.

January 2 – Sent Balacho to Chincha to the Feteraries & Cossah to Wobarah to take the mail to my darling. Still foggy – like rainy season.

January 3 – Clearing up. Sent Licka with a letter, strawberries & ground cherries. Failed to return today.

January 4 – Sat. About 10:30 my lover arrived home, alone – a prisoner of "Gultitas" enroute to Chincha. Hastily getting clean clothes & a little lunch, he went on, taking chlorodyne with him. Yesterday 50 to 60 natives came at 2:30, beating them all with sticks, throwing mud, etc. & taking them to Gulto as prisoners. "All things for the gospel's sake!" Hallelujah, got home for supper.

January 5 – Quiet

January 13 – Sun. Miss Bray read Jn. 15 in eve. Dirsita, Tiginia & bro. arrived at dusk. Good mail & a few supplies from A.A. John & Hal called on Tesima's father in Bailey in p.m. Sent Balacho to Fitawrari to get permission to take Miriam to Dr. R. He asked to see Hal immediately before we go.

January 14 – Hal & John called on Feterari who failed to see them saying he'd taken Coso. Liar! Sent message we couldn't go to Walamo, couldn't stay in Shama, must get home, get wife & kiddies & possessions & come <u>tomorrow morning</u> to "sit in Chincha." He refused our gift (tricycle).

January 15 – Hal & John went to Chincha to phone Mr. Ohman & Dejazmatch Makonnen. Tiginia left with a similar message at 2:30 a.m. Sewed & packed all day. Tired but resting in Christ. Hal was sick – nervous indigestion? Balacho's baby girl born last nite.

January 16 – Hal & John went to Chincha to rec. Mr. O message. Did not come.

January 17 – John & Hal went over Shamah Mt. to get a telegram from the Chincha man who had it for us (from Dejaz Makonen) & who came over to see the Gov's "guts." The rascal wouldn't bring it to us, here.

January 18 – 10 – 6 carries & 6 animals from Soddu came. Hal & J. off to Chincha with the telegram they got yesterday <u>for</u> the Feturari from Degaz Ma Konen. Unsatisfactory! Had to sign paper saying they wouldn't leave Shama except to go to Chincha. Prisoners! Free in the Lord, however & rejoicing in Him! Sent 2 Negadis to Soddu to intervene Gov.

January 19 – Large crowd attended Sun. services, 72. I'm very tired today. Had a sweet time preparing message for this evening – 123 Psalm. Sent Balacho to Chincha to send another phone call to Dijaz.

January 20 – Mon. Timcut. Balacho didn't return until tonite. Sent the message today.

January 21 – 10 carriers & Negadis & 6 mules still sitting.

January 23 – Miss Bray tells me (today) she fears that Miriam has either T.B. or a heart murmur. "Our God is our refuge & strength." The Walamos (sent back to get a traveling paper from the Walamo gov.) arrived at noon. That is good! (Digging a "dug-out" [hide out] for the missionaries at Soddu).

January 24 – Hal & John took the Digaz Ma Konnen's papers to Feturarie Shawin Giezow who refused to see them saying he'd taken medicine. What a rogue! God is able!! Negadis return to Soddu tomorrow. Hal & John are tired. Feturarie S. says for them to come in to see him again tomorrow.

January 25 – John sick today so he & Hal didn't take the telegram to Chincha as the Feturarie had said yesterday.

January 26 – Quiet Sun. Guntah Balabat called. 55 adults at a.m. service. John spoke on Jacob at our eve service.

January 27 – Heard this a.m. that Shawin Giezow was coming to Shama today to see his grain so all a.m. we watched for him to come. At 1 p.m. a mob arrived taking John & Hal prisoners, not allowing them to come into the house to change clothes to go to Chincha. Their messenger arrived late, so John & Hal slept in our tent in our yard guarded – slept –? Rather little, I fear. Servants frightened beyond words. Cossa & Baroga fled, Tola had an "accident," Corka was seized, etc.

January 28 – About 9:45 off to Chincha were taken my lover & John, also old Idiko (Corka was released here) with a great crowd, chain & all. How we are praying. 3 gabamias guard us here. Sent Tiginia to Soddu with a letter about this to Mr. O[hman]. Praise God, about 4 P.M. John & Hal returned having sent a phone message to Dr. Lambie with Fet. S.G. gave his consent to our going to Soddu, but is still ugly & deceitful.

January 29 – Toga & Bocula (of Chincha) spent much of the day here. Many neighbors came yesterday & today to "tàss 'ahi" us. Poor dear old souls! Their sympathy "gets" me. Hal is all broken up with the thot of having to leave these people with no messenger of the cross. John & Miss Bray are also packing expecting us all to be called to Walamo.

February 2 – Sun. Cossa did not arrive tonight.

February 3 – Word from Mr. Ohman with Cossah & negadis & carriers who came at 7:30 p.m. for all the Streets to come there [to Soddu] & for Miss Bray & John to remain. That didn't go down at all well with one of those concerned.

February 4 – Finished preparations for going to Soddu today. All ready tonight.

February 5 – Wed. Left home at 8:30 – arrived at Azo at 2 p.m. Rained during nite at Azo so my darling had to move his bed.

February 6 – Left Azo in the cold wind. Good to arrive in lower altitude & finally at Baroda. Otto Mususha's wife brot us eggs & milk. Animals slept in "big lady's" home.

February 7 – Friday. [Left] Baroda at 6:05 – reached Gulcho in due season.

February 8 – Left Gulcho in good season & safely arrived here, heartily welcomed by whites & blacks around 10 a.m. Tea at Ohmans, then M. Jr. B. & I at [Roberts'] & Hal & [Paul] at Ohmans'.

February 9 – Sun. My lover spoke in eve. Service. Miriam had an exam this a.m. No enlarged heart. Rheumatic fever continues. No lung trouble noticable now.

February 10 – Removed one finger nail for Miriam & one for Bobby this a.m. Hal had a tooth filled this p.m.

February 11 – Opened Bobby's ear (right) today.

February 12 – Re-opened Bobby's ear today.

February 13 – I attended women's mtg at Roberts & my lover looked after the kiddies. 26 women present.

February 14 – Telegram from Dr. Lambie asking if Hal & John were still prisoners. Opened both of Bobby's ears today.

February 15 – The Negadras came to dinner at Ohman's so the kiddies ate here. Hal was asked about the Gamo matter. Telegram from the British Legation asking if John was a prisoner.

February 16 – Sun. Had eve. service here, Mr. O. speaking. The 2 runners returned from A.A. – nothing definite. (Word from British legation requesting John's coming to Soddu.) This he desires to do as does Miss Bray.

February 17 – All the grown-ups had a happy time at the Ohman's this noon – "Watt & ingeria." My left eye seems sore & itchy.

February 18 – Ohman's wedding anniversary – 5th. Lovely dinner at Rs' – dominoes after & devotions. Soaking Bobby's & Miriam's fingers, Paul's leg & Hal's hand. My cold hangs on terribly.

February 19 – Tiginia returned – all quiet & peaceable. Shawin Giezow pretended to be friendly at least. Neither one of those there [John nor Miss Bray] wrote to us, but both wrote confidentially to Mr. Ohman. "All things," tho, somehow. Jr. running a temp of 101.2° tonight – thoro exam in eve. – also a beginning on me.

February 20 – Dr. finished examining me this p.m. Found Miriam's blood count was 10,000 (7,000 is right) so she had to be put to bed today to stay. Jr. has to remain, too – bad tonsils, so are also Paul's & Bobby's. Can't remove them until they get better.

February 21 – Rainy. Taking specimens from me these 24 hrs. (Later okay – thank the Lord!)

February 22 – My lover is busy packing his boxes to give them to the Negadis today. Mail (late). Also left here today.

February 23 – My lover brought a precious message tonight on "God's perfect man" Ps. 34. Communion followed. Mrs. R had all of our family here together & had my birthday cake. How kind, before my lover had to go!

February 24 – Jr's white count slightly sub-normal but O.K. At 6 a.m., my sweetheart left for home. Oh, how I wish we could all be going together. "All things," I know. May this separation soon be over if to His glory. All 3 kiddies were allowed to sit in sun 2 hours this a.m. after several days in bed.

February 25 – Paul stays on nicely at Ohman's. My lover should reach home today. 2 more hrs. sun for kiddies. Enid Forsberg's birthday.

February 26 – 2 hrs. sun for children. (It often rains these days & nights.)

February 27 – Roberts & Lois sang "Happy Birthday" at breakfast & opened a can of delicious pears for lunch in my honor. My own darling's note reached me at 6:30 a.m. & <u>that</u> was so precious. Bobby's ears had to be reopened – 6th time for one or other or both, – poor dear!

February 28 – Prayer Day. 2 carriers immed. after p.m. services bring our Oxandal pkge. Also word for Dr. R. to go to "war."

March 1 – Sun. Mr. Ohman spoke on Lev. offering "consecration" in eve. Good message – flat (apparent) results – trust not <u>really</u> so. Looked at Ray's map (Ethiopia) after & Italy's possible route, Sodamo via Gamo.?

March 2 – Reopened Bobby's right ear this eve. My lover should get his mail tonight. Tomorrow, he'll likely take Shawin Giezow his letter. How my heart goes out to him! I was thrilled to get his good letter via John (& Miss Bray) who arrived today.

March 3 – Hallelujah! Miriam's blood count is normal today so she does not have to stay longer in bed. She has another infected finger. Paul had his 1st sun treatment after thoro exam.

March 4 –Bobby's temp. has been normal all day. Also Miriam's continues to be. Paul's is sub- & Jr's ab. normal. A.A. Negadies arrived, also Ruth Quinn's pkge. The kiddies are so happy. My heart goes out to (& for) my darling tremendously. I'm longing for the mail to come <u>& him</u>!

March 5 – Tiginia with my precious one's mail came at supper time immediately followed by Mr. O. suggesting our home-going (to U.S.) immediately if full council agreed. Mr. Lewis to take over Gamo. What a shock, tho God has been speaking lately. No sleep until 1 a.m. to 5 this nite, I found later.

March 6 – Still in a quandary as to just what is best in regard to taking the kiddies, or what, to Gamo. Looking to the Lord. Today Mr. Lewis, Selma & four other girls were to sail from England. Looks as tho the Lord wants us to go now.

March 7 – Finished my letter to my sweetheart concerning it all today & gave it to Mr. Ohman. (Negadis, I now learn, are going in the a.m.)

March 8 – No service tonight as Ray is sick at Ohmans & Mrs. R. is, at R's. (She had a general anesthetic this a.m. in order to pull some teeth.)

March 9 – The negadis should reach Shama tonight with Mr. Ohman's & my letters to bring my lover up this week. May God prepare him for the message! (our home-going – U.S.)

March 11 – Writing many letters these days & am practically "caught up."

March 12 – Lest my sweetheart should be coming, & Fip is tired out, I sent Gub. & Tola out with Pax today. They returned with Togali & word that my lover is at Baroda tonite – tomorrow here!

March 13 – Sent Gub & Togalie with Pax to meet my darling. He arrived after 12 N., while we were at the noon-day station prayer meeting. In eve., he & I went to Ohman's so Hal & Mr. O. could discuss language. To bed late & my sweetheart is so tired. God graciously gave him a good trip & favorable weather on the way.

March 14 – Packing for Gamo – plan to leave Monday. Played dominoes in eve. at Ohman's. Ray, John T., Dr & Mrs. R., Lois, Miss Bray, Omans, Hal & I. Had a jolly time together.

March 15 – Sun. Eve. Service, John T. speaking, at the Ohman's – communion following with Hal officiating. (It was funny to see him trying to set down the communion table.) A sweet service.

March 16 – After tea (& all that accompanies leaving in Ethiopia) we left. I had to stay in bed all p.m. (after reaching camp at Gulcho) for nearly fainting repeatedly. Dr. R. was to leave for Denasin (war) this p.m.

March 17 – While very weak & hardly able to travel, Miriam had stomach aches enroute. The Lord undertook & I reached Baroda. Zebanya at B., very ugly – whole town out, but Hal very sick – swollen, itchy, blotchy poisoned – honey water, I think. Vomited, so that helps some.

March 18 – Hal is so exhausted & sick, being able to travel only because he must. Reached Azoh in "due season."

March 19 – How good to get home again – 11:45 a.m. Spent all the rest of the day greeting friends & neighbors who came to say, "God be praised, you have come again!"

March 20 – Rested as much as possible – many visitors, however. How I long for them to give our [Christ] such a reception!

March 21 – So tired!! We are <u>all</u> used up after trek.

March 22 – So good to have a quiet Sun. We are so tired we need it. Jr. is sick, vomiting. So did Paul during night, but okay today. Ababa Ferie 3½ hrs. – temp. negadras Chin.

March 23 – Mon. Junior, still sick & weak – can take milk only. Had a light supper & retained it, thank God.

March 24 – Cossa's & Artchie's baby girl came this eve. I spent some time down there today. How I wish I could help them! Poor souls.

March 25 – Hal & the "boys" prepared our "dug-out" down the hill under some berry bushes. Junior is better – still giving him chlorodyne. Hal typed our general letter – preparing folk at home.

March 26 – Junior has dysentery – giving chlorodyne & starch diet.

March 27 – Prayer Day! Rained hard (lightning & thick fog) this aft. & evening! Hard rains all last wk, & this, at nite.

March 28 – Balacho off – sick.

March 29 – Sun. Tiginia came early. Good mail. First funds for furlough. God is directing. I spoke in eve. – 143 Psalm. Bobby isn't quite himself. Jr. about well.

March 30 – How good it is to see Junior's feet in some shoes again!

March 31 – Bobby's temp 101.4. He is cutting 2 teeth. Whether it is tonsils, teeth or ears I do not know, but He does & to Him we look.

April 2 – Bobby is weary, but better, tho still carrying slight fever – teeth I think. He can hardly stand the thot of food & sleeps a great deal.

April 3 – Balacho still off sick. Killed our black cow – Tola (?) wasn't as distressed over his stealing some (meat) as I was.

April 4 – Bobby weighs only 25¼ lbs. as compared with 29 at Soddu. Hope he soon gets well.

April 5 – Balacho back at work, Guburo off – swollen glands. Miss B. read Jn. 12 for eve. Mail (boots, shoes & hats from England – Maude's nuts & candy via Selma – & many letters) arrived at 6 p.m. – also doz. oranges as a gift to the kiddies from Mr. Mitchell.

April 6 – Tola asked off today to be married tomorrow.

April 7 – Guburo is off still – sick.

April 9 – Tiny rain only – different from the hard rains we've had for a month almost. Went to Bailey – 10 a.m. till 4:00 P.M. There are no words to express my weariness, but I'm so thankful He enabled me to go. ("Gub" on duty today.)

April 10 – My lover spent the p.m. in Bailie. Tago is building his new house today.

April 11 – Tola off sick.

April 12 – Easter – Lovely Resurrection message my darling brot in evening meeting. Dark day & cold. Mail came – Paxton Xmas letters mostly.

April 13 – Tola returned today.

April 17 – Dietas tribe, Gulta Amharas, Wobaras etc at war.

April 18 – War continues. Shamas, Sharahs, etc. added – 18 dead so far – all Dieta houses burnt. Much concern. Miriam's head is being kerosened again today.

April 19 – Sun. Balacho only here, all other servants (but Cassah who didn't get home from Chincha market until noon today) went to war – 500 (?) men went over the upper path today – Walamo, Achols, Bailey & every country & tribe. Word from A.A., Cassa says to leave only the ashes of Deita & Bonkie "soul." Balacho went at noon. Mail came at 4:30 P.M. I spoke on "The Fixed Heart." F.C. [Field Council] decision disappointing.

April 20 – Tabech is our house servant today – all others at the war. Bal. back at noon, driving an ox as his booty. We weren't slow expressing our disapproval. Writing to Mr. O. for advice concerning our furlough plans. Mr. & Mrs. O., due here Apr. 30.

April 21 – Dismissed Tabech tonite as Tola & Guburo returned this a.m. My lover studies practically <u>all</u> the time in preparation for his language exam.

April 22 – "Fired" Togalie this a.m. on his return. Burogo hasn't yet come back. War over, seemingly. God reminds me tonite we are not to look to man in our dilemma, via daily light.

April 25 – After dark Tushodi, Locka, Waldie came, eve. having sent for servants due to ours having deserted to go to the great tribal war in Wabaros & Deta. They have now returned & are greatly disturbed over the arrival of others, thinking their jobs insecure, possibly.

April 26 – Quiet Sun. Miss Bray read 147 & 148 Ps. in the eve. Odio (Walamo) arrived this morning.

April 27 – Ohman's were to have left Soddu today to come to Shama to take our place. We are to leave the foll'g Mon. <u>No</u> funds, but God!! May He quickly intervene.

April 29 – Packed our trunks today, even some trek things in the hand trunks.

April 30 – Miriam, Jr. & Hal went out to meet Mr. & Mrs. O. who reached here late in the a.m. Paul has a very lame ankle – poison in system or sprain (??) Let Tola & Guburo go as they won't go to A.A.

May 1 – Tiginia arrived in the middle of the forenoon. We are to stay a little, at least, (letter from Mr. Duff) as Dessie has been taken & A.A. warned so Dr. Lambie feels it unsafe for any others from South to go to Addis. God is leading, He isn't failing or faithless & He will direct our steps. Negadis & carriers (ours for A.A. trek) will go back to Soddu with the Ohman's.

May 2 – Played dominoes in eve. to help Mr. Ohman & my darling "unlax" – they are working so hard on language. Mr. O. is very hoarse.

May 3 – Sun. My lover spoke in eve. service. Had Ohman's & Miss B. for dinner & supper.

May 4 – My lover and Mr. O. spent the day signing up land owners & going to Desta to Tiginia's wife's, getting home at 5 P.M. wet. Streams high. Miss B. still wants to go to Soddu.

May 5 – Ohman's left in the fog at 8:30 a.m.

May 7 – Guburo got "beaten-up" by the Gulta Amharas for being our servant – eggs broken, hand swollen, etc.… Cossa brot 5 bananas as gersha tonite.

May 8 – Working diligently on children's school work these days. Much rain & fog. Bobby gets his ears syringed daily – he is pale. My darling spends all his time on lang. & translation.

May 17 – Mail! Word that Messrs. Mitchell & [Devers] were killed in Asusie desert – A.A. taken [by the Italians] 5/6 after Haille Selassie [the Ethiopian Emperor] fled to Palestine 5/5. Dr. Lambie injured –

26 [Gamans] etc. killed in A.A. Soddites are barricading & the Gebanias guarding them. I [wait] peace in our eve. service. "But God."

May 18 – My darling went to see the Chincha negadras who discounts all this – ???, but was very kind, grateful & reassuring.

May 19 – My lover, Junior & I went to Dorsey – a great play day. Such sights! I nearly passed out on the hills. Came home in rain & fog arriving at 5:35. Left soon after 1 P.M.

May 20 – Weary after yesterday's jaunt but the Dorsey's greatly appreciated our interest shown by our going visit. Didn't take cold, fortunately Stiff!

May 21 – Boys terribly upset – Miss B's propaganda seemingly. All neighbors distressed, too, telling us we are to be killed & kiddies, stolen! <u>God</u>! <u>He</u> is our sufficiency!

May 22 – Balacho & Tushodie went to Dokho to get negadis. Walamo boys afraid to stay. Miss B. insists on going so Hal & I have decided there's no alternative, but to leave in the nite tonite. Packing & preparing. Put kiddies to bed in clothes. Boys returned – no negadies, thank God! All p.m. prayed they wouldn't come. We <u>don't</u> want to run away & leave all our tack here, but war will come surely "except God!"

May 23 – Sun. I spoke using "His Riches" – Harrison as basis. Bal's father-in-law came urging us not to leave – saying people wanted our goods & money, not our lives. The very air is charged!

May 24 – Tarafo's father & others afraid our kiddies are to be stolen. Much weeping by the many who came to share our trial. God! May <u>He</u> triumph yet.

May 25 – Tues. My darling & I did <u>all</u> we could to persuade Miss Bray <u>not</u> to start off to Walamo – in vain. At noon, Dokho negadies came – she left, a hold-up gang raided her things & our home. Guns pointed at us repeatedly, but God! But God! In evening, Cow

Chulties & Abogodis & crowd came to "zebanya" us – during nite stole <u>everything</u> from Miss B's house.

May 26 – Wed. During heavy fog, I saw same crowd "clean out" the tukel. Old Garcho has our trunk & blankets & hand bags, but they waylaid him & his wife. Balacho & Gultas came bringing a few articles they'd taken from "cow chutdies" crowd. Somebody stole our lot of keys, broke stable lock, so animals are in our yard. Bal's father-in-law "umpta the biaras" to me. Hump! Got out our animals to flee. Tago fled. Miss B. went on. Dorsey Zebanyas blew horn & dashed over the hill. Hal & I decided to stay. Miss B. very angry because we sent 2 men to bring her back. Gulta women came to carry off our things, saying "Tassa, Tassa!"

May 27 – Dressed heavily & never removed money belts even at night. Everything so tense! Dorsey's staid all nite, blowing horn every little while. 3 nites in much less than a wk. with no sleep (to mention.) Very much used up, Hal & I both. God – He is our all. If our lives can be used to bring these people to [Christ], we gladly lay them down, the kiddies included. Chincha crowd came asking if we wanted zebanyas. Very hard days & nights. God keeps the kiddies marvelously.

May 28 – Fri. My darling was escorted (under guard) to Feturari Danya's this p.m. Heavy guard here. Dorsey zebanyas sent home by Chincha crowd. Fet. Danya asked us to come to Chincha (thru his head man), but Hal told him how bad that would be so he has, at the "big man's" suggestion, gone to confer with Fet. Danya. He asked us to remain until this affair has been cleared up before going to Walamo.

May 29 – I continue to act as zebanya. Togo has been up & down 4 times (from Balu) – much goods returned today – all p.m. Hal rec'd it, made notations & got thumb prints. Miss B. & I had a few unkind words in kitchen, "but God!" Togo's baby boy born in eve.

May 30 – Sun. My lover spoke on Job's chastening – Reassuring & profitable to us just now. Many came & went today – no time for rest or privacy. Kiddies have colds & Junior complains of his tonsils. Cows came home (Sat. I think).

May 31 – My darling at 8:45 A.M. had to go to Chincha – getting home at 4 P.M. simply soaking wet. Togo had to go to Dorsey church due to death of an Amhara woman from Bailey. World news – Germany, by nite, took Rome. I wonder what really is authentic – whether Italy, England, or Germany has taken Ethiopia. Balacho & father-in-law came over in a.m. Gub scared!

June 1 – Making sleeping bags yesterday & today for the road & getting tent ropes into the fly. Washed my hair. Eldo came over & Miss B. gave him a few things. Chincha Bocula's wife came wanting to have a tooth extracted. No forcepts. Togo brot us 11 eggs. Zebanyas still on duty. Tenseness is lifting. May God be glorified. Feturari Danya is due here on Thursday. May God direct! <u>Only His will</u>, we desire. After dark, Tushodie Waldies & 2 other Walamos arrived bringing letter from Mr. Ohman. Phone call came thru from him at 5 p.m. also. "How many mules we want?" Killed a cow for Balec people this afternoon.

June 2 – My darling spent all day in Chincha trying to get in touch (by phone) with Mr. Ohman. He's to go in again at 9 a.m. to talk to him then (in the a.m.). Very quiet day here – washed & got dry all the clothes. Feturari Danya – urges us to remain until all is settled. Thiefs have taken to the "low country." One bag full of clothes (Miss B.'s) returned & 3 M.T.'s to Chinca Bocula which Hal brot home last nite. Zugie Dorsey gave us a sheep. He promises mules & zebanyas for our going to Soddu. F. Danja, [Italian] soldiers saying mules all lost in war. May our Father soon direct – make plain our path for His glory. Much trouble in Walamo due to Wal.-Marrako war.

June 3 – My lover left at 7:30 for Chincha. Returned at 4 P.M. – unable to get Mr. O. – thinks the "Silktenya" is waiting for a "gusha." Zugie (of Dorsey) offered to loan us money, up to 200 M.T.'s if desired. Declined. All quiet here all day. Dismissed Hile – bad egg! Few more articles returned to Miss B. – also my leather coat & $1 M.T. to us – promise of more tomorrow.

June 4 – My lover left at 7:30 for Chincha again, hoping to get in touch with Mr. O. Today. Tushodie & another Walamo left with a letter. Waldie & Daya staid here. Beautiful sunrise. No rain yesterday, praise the Lord. Later – no rain at all today which ought to help take away kiddies colds & sore tonsil trouble. Hal got back a little before 2 P.M. Hadn't gotten Mr. O. Rec'd a few more articles & $1 M.T.

June 5 – Before devotions were over this a.m., Bocula, of Chincha came asking Miss B. to go to Chincha to see a woman who was shot last night. She consented if Hal or I would go, too, so he went, first sending Togalie to "Zugies" to ask him to come here tomorrow or Mon. instead of today as he had expected to. Kiddies playing out-of-doors – cool, but sunny. Hal & Miss B. returned 4 p.m. Woman will die – bullet in abdomen.

June 7 – Mon. Phone call completed. Mules are to leave Soddu Thursday to take us there. Tsugie came this eve. Very kind.

June 10 – Balacho came asking Hal to go to Gamo to get the $10 that crowd demanded. Wrote a paper in reply asking to have it to be brot here. Gub. off sick.

June 11 – Baroga quit today. "Gub." is back. Tangie & Bocula due at 8 a.m. to make (completed packing) final arrangements with the station. Beautiful day – kiddies still have colds, but they are better.

June 12 – Another Chincha & Dorsey trip for Hal. Bocula & Sugre returned with him, papers written & signed by Tago & others as witnesses. Completed packing except for "last min." things.

June 16 – Kiddies still sick with colds – keeping them in bed often these days.

June 17 – Walamo arrived early this aft. – no Wal. negadis willing to come.

June 18 – Discovered today we have been right as far as the days of the week are concerned, but are date behind. For instance, we thot this was the 17th. All 6 Walamo boys to leave early in a.m. for Soddu. Much trouble there between Govs. & Kings men – each demanding all, threatening to rob Frangies, etc. Dayo wants to work for us – asked me about a wk ago. Nobody wants to work for Miss B. My lover spent the day in Dorsey & Chincha – no chance to leave this way. Somehow I feel it to be God's will for us just to sit & wait. So does Hal. "Gub." is off – sore foot. Beautiful sun all p.m. Heavy fog all a.m.

June 19 – Fri. Bobby's right ear began to drain. He cried much last night. Surely God is our Refuge & He will not fail. "Gub" back today. He, Tarkely & Cossa now only serve now. Very little wood. Barely enuf for each day. Made arrangements with Gutamah's mother to bring milk again, beginning tomorrow. Made Bobby's birthday cake. Foggy almost all day.

June 20 – Sat. Fetuari Danya here for lunch. Sugie arriving before he left – each hate & distrust the other. After Sugie ate (beans & spinach, coffee & bread) his Zebanyas searched several houses finding some things. Cold & foggy.

June 21 – Sun. Cold & foggy all day. Fet. Danya asked Hal to go to Gulta today so he spent the day there. Balacho's father-in-law sent a lamb to me – sin – sin – trying to "bribe" me, no doubt, remembering how he asked me for the "bērȧs." Eldo was here in a.m. Bobby greatly enjoyed his birthday cake, eating off the raisins & candy trimmings. "Tabash" was here for cake & lime drink, too.

June 22 – My lover discovered yesterday while at Fet. Danya's that Takalie & Guburo hadn't gone near Gulta with the paper to the man who has our $10 M.T's. Sugie wanted them to go so my darling sent them. Gub. returned that eve. with the story that Takalie was tied up, etc. etc. All lies. These servants have a hard task mastering Satan. Had a hard time drying the washing. My darling brot a gun from

Sugies where he went today. Cossa is to be zebanya, moving up to Balacho's house tomorrow. Borana & bro. are to live at stable.

June 23 – Tues. Fetuari Danya is reported to be accepting bribes from those caught by Sugie with our goods. Oh, what sin! Beautiful sunshine all day. Washed my hair, drying it in the sun. Kiddies better, praise God. My lover has had an aching right shoulder blade for a wk. Cool, these days.

June 25 – One month since our 1st raid. Hal & I have lost many pounds, but what does that matter. We experience constantly both the peace of God & the God of peace & that is enough, praise His holy Name!

June 26 – Prayer Day. Takalie & Gub. heard today what Fetuari Danya told us last Sat. – many Italians had entered Walamo taking guns, etc. Walamo boys haven't yet returned, being gone a week today. Cold, foggy, damp, & miserable weather yesterday & today.

June 28 – Sun. Quiet, rainy day. Before supper, Dayo, Waldie carriers, and negadis came. We are to leave, D.V., Tues. for Soddu. My darling has a cold.

June 29 – Preparing to leave tomorrow. Many have come to tell us how they regret our departure! May they learn to know <u>Him</u> soon!

June 30 – Sugie didn't come today to take our things so we will leave in the a.m. as he is to come then. My lover went to Chincha & Dorsey to get things finished so we could go.

July 1 – Couldn't leave until 11 a.m. Reached Ago (& camped) at 5 P.M. Rained & much fog, but we aren't very wet. So tired I couldn't sleep for hrs.! I'm carrying so much "extra weight."

July 2 – Waldo Guba (nagadie) is terribly slow every day – 8:20 this a.m. when we left – clear day & sunny. Pax was terrible! falling on my darling (with Bobby) 3 times breaking his glasses, wearing him out badly. Reached Baroda (& camped) at 2 P.M. Good (though weary) day. Friends brot supplies.

July 3 – Rained – left camp at 11:15 a.m. Reached Gulcha at dusk – very friendly there to us, bringing corn & milk & camping in "head-man's" yard. Put kiddies immed. in bed – took them drinks & milk & lime juice (no supper), rest more necessary. By the time I cooked breakfast, etc & got to bed, it was 10 P.M. So tired!

July 4 – Everything we own is soaked thru & thru, whether on us, our animals, or in boxes, but we are so grateful to God for bringing us into Soddu safely (2:30 P.M.) Yesterday & today the men went out to meet us, but we were late in reaching here. The rivers are all high. "Sue" nearly drowned. It has rained <u>all</u> day. We are sleeping tonight in our new home here – nurses residence. All so tired.

July 5 – Too tired to move today, but managed to get thru. Went to bed in eve. rather than to mtg., which I wanted to attend. Raining, but not cold.

July 6 – Washed – rainy in a.m., but clothes dried a little in the p.m.

July 7 – Sunshine – how good it is for the dear children. Enid's appendectomy this a.m. All went well.

July 8 – <u>Many</u> former Walamo friends have come to welcome us here & to express their sympathy over Gamo experiences. <u>Much</u> typhus about us.

July 9 – Many "big men" are coming here to decide whether to resist those advancing from south. Conflicting reports. Italians or English?? My, I hope, the latter. Baily men on horse, with a white feather in their hair & "trophies" on the horses bridle, go past here, returning from Marrakko war – they have killed a man. Women are split open – cut up & left to die by the roadside.

July 10 – My lover has so much pain in "gall bladder region & right shoulder blade that sleep is interrupted & so he is weary, thin, too. He's helping at the hospital this wk! I weigh 126 now – 21 pds less than 1 yr. ago.

Ababa Feri & Mr. Hatchik called this p.m. Served Tea! Sent a letter to those at Lambuda by Ababa F's friend.

July 11 – 1 wk. ago we arrived – we've been all wk. getting our things dried out from our trip up here. Washed 3 days this wk. trying to get caught up & get the road mud cleaned out. Mended & ironed this eve. while my lover finished reading Orr's book thru Canada.

July 12 – At noon, Paul expressed great fatigue. I quickly gave him his dinner & put him to bed. He had a long sleep, but he felt very weary when he got up at 4:15. I gave him his supper & put him to bed at 6 P.M. Took his temp. 102.³, so called Dr. R. He can find no reason now for that so will have to see what develops. Hal has the eve'g service. I staid home with the kiddies.

July 13 – Paul in bd all day – temp 99.²

July 14 – Paul allowed up about middle of a.m. – temp normal. What caused his illness, we still do not know.

July 15 – Ray, Mr. Ohman & Hal put glass in front door late, after finishing similar work at hospital. Fiturari Gumie arrived today – much shooting to welcome him.

July 16 – A great company of "big" men went up our road as we finished dressing this a.m. Mr. O, Mal F. & my lover called on Dejaz Mekonnan this a.m. Gusha of tomatoes & corn today. God supplies!

July 31 – My darling was sick practically all night. At 3:30 a.m. I called Dr. – seemingly gall stones. He's weak, tired & sore today & must stay in bed & avoid heavy work for a long time, Dr. says.

August 1 – Had Dr. & Mrs. Roberts & Lois for dinner (Mrs. R. making Miriam's birthday cake.) & Miriam invited Enid & Mal to tea. (they brought her some good sugared popcorn) So in all, she had a happy 10th birthday, the dear little girl!

August 2 – Sent Goffa postman with 1 letter from each person here, hoping they got out via Kenya & English army. My lover still is upset after his hard time Thurs. night. Too bad, poor dear.

August 8 – My darling & Mr. Ohman went to see Kanamatch Sugil – found him at Lidg Johannes in solitary confinement & pretty sick.

August 9 – Miriam vomited during the night, but seems ok today. I went to p.m. prayer meeting – my lover went to the evening service. Mal spoke. Beautiful, warm p.m. after a.m. of clouds and a little rain. How different from Gamo. Bocula Shofta & Fitawrari Danya returned to Chincha today. The Fitawrari sent us a big sheep recently. Ababa Ferie sent 75 bananas the middle of the week. Quiet, restful Sunday.

August 10 – Daya off at a weeping – supplied a sub, however. I have an ugly cold still & am so achy all the time. At noon mail from Mr. Pinkgrass came bringing some Addis Ababa news, the 1st since Ohman's were at Soddo early in May. This provides a way to get a few letters by way of the Nile, thru British at Gore. Mental victory this p.m. for me – so fatigued am I. Wrote to Katherine.

August 12 – John Phillip's birthday.

August 28 – Put Miriam to bed, endeavoring to get rid of her bad cold & cough.

August 30 – John spoke tonite – Elijah – good.

September 2 – Mal & Enid left early this a.m. for their home in Gafia.

September 3 – At 2:30 a.m. an airplane came from southeast flew over here to Soddo, back east over desert road to Sidamo, over here again & back to Sidamo and disappeared. The harbinger of spring, Praise God. Daya forced a drunken Amhara out of our living room who was demanding quarters to take cover. Dr. examined Bobby, Junior & me this forenoon. I must get 1½ hrs. of rest each afternoon. Very tired heart. My nerves are frazzled, so weary. I'll stay in bed resting today. I couldn't help wishing that I could stay several days so I wouldn't be so hard on my precious family. Christ went <u>all</u> the way – so will I, by His grace!

September 6 – 2 wks. today since Sue was shot. Praise God, the kiddies didn't develop anything after her bites. The bites were burnt with nitric acid.

September 7 – 2 planes down by Hurnbo & lake today at noon, natives report. My lover had eve. Service – good spirit, he said. Miriam is still in bed with her cough & cold. My darling's bad (left shoulder) pain is better.

September 9 – Dr. gave Junior ether yesterday p.m. & pierced his ears. He & Miriam have colds as do I. (I stayed in bed all day today.)

September 10 – Jimma post arrived bringing also a letter to Miss Bray from Miss Cable & one to everyone here (addressed to Mrs. Roberts) from Selma.

September 12 – Wrote a note on the letters waiting here for Kathrine & Aunt Minnie so they could be mailed in the a.m. via Jimma.

September 13 – Sun. Paul, Miriam & Jr. are now all in bed. My cold is better, but it is like grippe that we all have.

September 21 – Opened Junior's ears again this p.m. giving ether which he took without any trouble. Dr. says to prepare for Jr's tonsillectomy next Thurs.

September 23 – Bobby is so weak – took him to the clinic and Dr. opened both ears (which were very bad.) Carried him home to bed. Gave Junior his final preparations for tomorrow. After supper Dr. came to say Ray had to have his appendectomy in a.m., so Jr. is postponed – all things. Dr. said today, as soon as Bobby is able & Jr. gets over his tonsillectomy, he will go through all of the kiddies – tonsillectomies. We are glad for that word, having hoped for that for some time.

September 24 – Ray got along nicely. Bobby doesn't like to be kept in bed, so keeps us busy trying to keep him quiet & happy.

September 25 – Prayer Day – I attended in the a.m. & Hal in p.m.

September 26 – Hal, Paul, Miriam, & Ohman's & Mal went to see Muschol play. Gov. invited them inside, but soon suggested that it was now time to go – thus preventing them from seeing the heathen customs.

September 27 – 12 precious, blessed years of joy & sweet fellowship together. Had station prayer meeting here with tea before. Mrs. Roberts made a delicious cake with orange blossoms & pink petals and a spray for me to wear. John T., Webb's, Johannes had dinner with us. Johannes is sick. Hal & I both went to the evening service where Hal spoke on Deut. 8.

September 28 – All station invited to Gutanas' for watt.

September 29 – Johannes very sick. Miriam, Paul & I went to Tushodies for cocha-cocha (very good, too) this noon with the others here at Soddo.

September 30 – Today we learned Dr. thinks Johannes illness from Sue's bite. We heard him crying out many times last nite. Poor lad. Johannes died at 4:00.

October 1 – Johannes funeral at 10 a.m. Mr. Webb is staying with us since last night. John is at Ohman's. Junior is better, praise God!

October 2 – Early this a.m., Mr. Ohman & Dr. came in saying I needed to go to the Roberts' for a rest. Bobby is to go to Ohman's. My lover feels sick, an attack (gall stones) is near. Junior is all right again.

October 3 – Mrs. Ohman is having a birthday party for Paul at 3 p.m. At 11 a.m. I went to bed at Roberts – low blood pressure, anemia, appendix sore, and the heart is the main thing. My lover didn't sleep at all 'til 4 a.m. – sick – small stone likely – nauseated and sore. Bobby went to Ohman's after lunch.

October 4 – Sun. Both services at Ohman's so that I would be quiet here. My lover has eaten nothing since last night. (He has eaten very little for a couple of days, the lover!)

October 5 – Peach & orange trees in Roberts' yard are blooming – so fragrant.

October 6 – Many soldiers returning from Lambuda. About 4 p.m. news came that all Lambuda Frangies are at entina Kala today & will get here tomorrow. Little orphan children like Bobby & Junior, being brot here as well as cattle & sheep. Oh how terrible is Satan and his power.

October 7 – Mr. Ohman, Mr. Webb & Dr. went to meet those from Lambuda – all arrived about noon. Today is five months fleeing. Praise God for their deliverance & safe arrival. He is so good. Hallelujah! 4 p.m. – Station praise & prayer meeting at Roberts'.

October 8 – Dr. opened Henry Phillips ears this a.m. & Bobby's this p.m. – the poor darlings. Hundreds & hundreds have passed today going home to Gamo from Lambuda war, with their spoils – women, children, animals, household things, trophies tied in clothes, hanging from their spears or horses' heads. Poor little kiddies, being sold for $1 or $2 for slaves.

October 9 – Jimma mail about 11 a.m. Father Street went to be with the Lord (Selma writes) early in July. Our Aug. 13th letters arrived in Addis Ababa & Selma wrote in reply Sept. 14 – getting here today. Fitawraris Guballi & Danya called on me this morning.

October 10 – Postman left at 4 p.m. Bobby's temp is 100, (Dr. opened one ear) refusing food – only 1 cup of milk was taken. Stopped taking digitalis today (took 1½ grams 2 times a day for over a month.)

October 11 – Sun. Both services at Ohman's on my account, 'tho my pulse is lower tonight than formerly in evening. Bobby's temp 101 – both ears draining. Dona Salata's brot Gamo corn for supper – good.

October 12 – My lover had a poor night, (gall stone) attack is near – my darling what a time he has, but God. How good! Read Addis mail to Jimma folk – so kind of them to share them with us. Word of home-going of Mrs. C. Cary & Mrs. Ralph Norton. I'm glad if God should call my sweetheart. I'd be happy to follow soon, too. D.V. However that is in His hands as is everything that concerns us

& we are glad indeed to leave it there. Mr. Trout doubtless will soon go, too. Cancer, Dr. Roberts says. Yes, heaven gets nearer every day. How one longs for the time when we shall all be gathered there!

October 13 – Tues. Finished "Jungles Preferred" by Dr. Janet Miller, Riverside Press – Cambridge, Mass. Bobby darling's ears still draining. Washed Junior's today too as they hurt.

October 14 – Bobby's temp 100 still in bed – ears draining. Paul eats very little & is constantly weary. I began to take a new medicine, iodine for my glands. Lois said that it caused my pulse rate to lower and I am improving. Praise God, I am having fewer fluttering heart spells, aches, and lack of breath feeling. May I continue, God willing!

October 15 – Bobby's temp – 100. Miss Bray's birthday (51). I sat up on the porch 1 hr. with no ill effects. Hal went to believers' mtg. with Mr. Ohman in p.m. Junior's ears seem all right now. Hal is trying to talk up the Bible Conference, but Mr. Ohman feels that most are too busy.

October 16 – Up 1½ hrs – weary – so I went back to bed. Praise God – home mail, 1st since April – 2 from Maude – May 23, July 14, Katherine June 14, Ethel June 4.

October 17 – Mail left – request for plane included – Bobby continues to improve slowly. Squabble between Walamo tribe & Amharas near Maraks. Word (rumor) that probably that the Samdies & Italians are only one long day's journey from here. How we hope it is true. God's will we want & His protection. He is enough. Sent letters to Maude and Ethel, Katherine, Selma, Mrs. Jefferies. Up 2 hrs. today, with ¾ hr. in between.

October 18 – Up in a.m. for ¼ hr. for a tub bath. Back to bed until dinner time – up then 2 hrs. including ½ hr. at home with my lover. Up again between 8 & 9 p.m. for communion. My darling is sick – stone?

October 19 – My lover is so tired and weak – in bed nearly all day. Ray had more nausea and pain in p.m. Bobby is well, Lois says. It is now general information that "Italian ashrais" are near – Dana Salata says they are to be allowed a "peaceable entrance". I had a thorough exam at the clinic. Dr. found, uterus is same condition as it was 2 years ago (large – soft & tipped) with something painful behind it. It might be an ovary dropped down. Blood pressure was up 10 pts making it 110 – it ought to be 127 for me. Because of draining, silver was applied inwardly.

October 20 – Walamos still returning with empty spears from Armassie. Ray and my lover are both still sick, but better. In the evening, Hal weak, but nausea was gone – so sore. I was up 2 hrs. in a.m. & another 2 in p.m., having a tub bath, & Lois washed my hair. Bobby's temp is up again 100+, the dear. Learned today that Sugie was sent home as a prisoner when Feterarie Gubalie went.

October 21 – My lover is better today – so am I – up 4 good hrs. Heard in a.m. from 3 town forangies & from Dana Solata that on Mon. & Tues. Yerger Alum was bombed & entered by Italians and that they would be here in 4 or 5 days. Heard from Salate that the Gofa natives & A's are fighting against each other. Shafara said in evening Dejaz Makonen may send down troops. Bobby is still sick – other kiddies are fair.

October 22 – At about 5:30 Dona Solata came from Gibby telling us tents are at the Balatie & the Italians will be here in 1 or 2 days. In evening Dola Negadras (Kala man) came, saying one of his men got in here today bringing the word that the Italians are this side of his home in Dola. I was up 4 hrs. today – a little weary tonight. My lover is all right now this p.m. Ray was up. I'm enjoying Bucham's "New Frontiers in Central Sudan" these days.

October 26 – Mon. Oh how happy I am to get home to stay today.

October 27 – Brought Bobby home this a.m. He is pale and so thin. Ears still being syringed daily.

November 2 – Had a delightful station surprise birthday supper at Ohman's for Peg. We played games later – lovely time.

November 8 – My lover had another dreadful attack today. Bobby was prepared today for his tonsillectomy in the morning.

November 9 – Dr. Roberts tried to do Bobby's tonsillectomy today, but Bobby stopped breathing, twice. Artificial respiration restored him. Dr. & Mrs. Roberts and Lois were so disturbed. Hal had to go back to bed afterward.

November 10 – My lover is still weak. Bobby is, too, although he had a good nite. I'm worn out.

November 11 – Bobby has dysentery – so sick. Dr. is alarmed at Bobby's weakened condition. For him to have this is bad.

November 12 – Dr. is giving Bobby Yatrine for a week. Dr. Quitenham brought it from Sidamo – Thank God!

November 13 – My darling had a light attack while attempting to clean the storeroom.

November 14 – 4 beautiful planes came today. Flew over here on to town, etc. Heard later 6 visited Lambuda & dropped papers – none here – although reported a bag of mail for Gov. was dropped, which he denied.

November 15 – My lover had another gall stone attack today – the poor dear.

November 16 – My sweetheart is still in bed.

November 17 – Had a lovely birthday tea for Henry Phillips at Ohman's for the kiddies and mothers. Jimma post came about noon, nothing from Addis Ababa for anyone here. Bomber planes are heard daily.

November 18 – Were paid some today up to Nov. 14. $30 and $2 more for horse. Had Cochi-Cochi at noon. Hal is better – had a good night.

November 19 – Mail left – due to another attack of my sweetheart, I only wrote to P. B. & Mildred & asked her to make carbons & send to LaSalle, Paxton, Dad, Ethel & Roy Wrights.

November 20 – Bobby is again well, thank God.

November 22 – My lover had a terrible attack – followed by leg ache and pain which lasted 2 or 3 days – the precious, poor darling.

November 23 – Sunday. The Dr. pronounced "Scarlet fever" in Miriam's case. Put her to bed. Moved Jr. in with Paul & Allen. He's not sick. Heard planes this morning at 10:00.

November 24 – Miriam's cheeks appeared quite flushed today – rash is still evident and her tongue is coated. She is not feeling too bad, however.

November 26 – Thanksgiving Day. Truly our Father cares for us. We had a can of salmon that I had saved for today since last December. Peg sent over 2 pumpkin pies. In the evening we had a time of singing. We heard blasting this morning while the Dr. was dressing Paul's burned ankle.

November 27 – Prayer day. We had our sessions here at home alone.

November 28 – Mail came at breakfast time. Easter letters and Christmas cards came together (mail from Mar., April, July & Oct.) Answers came in response to our general letters sent in August.

November 29 – Quiet Sunday here alone. Miriam's rash is entirely gone & her tongue is clear. Praise God! Gov. caught and is holding our postman and mail. Mr. Ohman & Ray called on Gov. The mail was released, but not the postman. Gov. fears that the Amhara's may be sending messages to the Italians in Jimma via this fellow. Zillah is in bed again today.

December 5 – Thrills! Before 11 a.m. a biplane arrived, flew all around here & town, returned here swinging around low over our house, men waving to us, etc. leaving by Sidamo (native version) wanted to land but we "tonssid them". Miriam began to peel today on her thighs. Junior & Paul asked if this was the plane we are praying for? Gurrios very frightened – never saw a plane before.

December 6 – Quiet & blessed Sunday. In evening my lover spoke on the Tabernacle as a type of believer (fresh, beautiful and helpful). Miriam has spent two weeks in bed.

December 7 – Sifted 2 bags of flour today – wormy & buggy – came from the Greek Giorges shop in town, but oh how thankful we're to have it.

December 8 – We're trying to "figure out" a few Christmas gifts these days for the kiddies. Allen is making toy guns, horses, etc.

December 12 – Paul's burn has finally healed. Miriam's blood count is better, now 12,000 as against 17,000.

December 13 – Allan spoke from Hosea – good.

December 14 – Have made & am completing ducks, dolls, p. g's, aprons for Christmas out of old clothes.

December 15 – Tobeck came from Gamo. Allan's board paid to Jan. 2, horse too. Amhara women, children, & goods fled. Is reported that the Italians will soon be coming. May they!

December 16 – Rumors afloat that natives desire to loot the station. We are at peace, however. My lover had a slight attack last night.

December 19 – John Truwin has scarlet fever. Ray is living outside in his tent & being nurse.

December 20 – A plane came this forenoon, flying low over our station & dropping a paper of greetings & salutations to us. I spoke tonight on Luke 2. Gov. sent us all an ox.

December 21 – Quiet day. Town foranges came asking permission to come and stay here – 35 town houses have been burned.

December 22 – Mr. A. – A.M.M's big man & Jacobs went to Gov. for permission to come here. Not granted. Gov. was a bit curt. Another plane today.

December 23 – Another plane today Bomber 1 & Bomber 2. Coming often now, dropping papers.

December 24 – Another plane today – more papers. Christmas Eve. & truly the Prince of Peace is filling us with joy and peace. Had servants' wives for supper. We shared the Christmas message and played.

December 25 – A precious day, filled with His joy. Lovely little packages in a stocking for each dear kiddie, plus all of Allan's good work made it a happy day for all. Rained – no planes.

December 26 – No planes – reported Gov. is going to put up a white flag. Henry has Scarlet Fever. John is in a tent outside.

December 29 – From 9:15 to 10:00 a.m. 3 planes were here – Amharas shooting at them. (The 1st planes since last Thursday.) Apparently no white flag, since machine guns were shot at times. 3 bombers bombed B1-B2-B4 in late p.m. around 4:30.

December 31 – Thurs. 3 bombers came at 4:40 and bombed.

Chapter 6

1937, Soddo, Addis Ababa, and the Return

January 4 – Same 3 bombers dropped many bombs near Gibe at 4:15.

January 6 – Roberts' want to flee. Dr. told Mr. O. to get up. Dona Selata offers to take us to [Italian] camp tonight. Praying for God's guidance.

January 8 – Another gall stone attack.

January 9 – A plane dropped a pkge. of mail here to be sent to Dejaz Makonen. Swooped low, scaling each house. Flag flown field downward – "Distress." My lover had a bad attack at noon yesterday, also has dysentery so have Alen and I.

January 10 – Quiet Sun. – precious eve. service – my lover – "golden altar, etc." Dejaz Makonen left for Sidamo – peace. afraid "Pop"a. has scarlet fever. 21000 blood count. (Later – false alarm, Thank God.)

January 11 – Quiet day – many A's gone to Sidamo, also W's. Fet. Zumie in charge here. Dolo Zebanya & Makabo keeping guard here somewhat. Fangie Zebarrias still "on." God guards – peace is ours, entirely.

January 12 – Plane dropped papers. Ibota off sick, Buna as sub. Miriam & Junior moved back into their room.

January 13 – Completely exhausted today – Heart & body. Buna off sick – whole population is sick with scarlet fever & dysentery – Frangies included pretty much. Disposing of our goods today.

January 14 – Couldn't get up today – so exhausted – in spite of the fact that the Italians & A's are due in today, rumor says. Feast at Gibbe is being prepared. Later – they didn't show up. Had a talk with Lois and told her of the trouble here. May God heal! Praying all day for her while in bed.

January 15 – Planned to stay in bed today, did so until around 9 or so when my darling became so nauseated & doubled up gall trouble that he had to go to bed. Alen & I worked the remainder of the a.m. with him. Dr. gave him 2 needles.

January 18 – My lover had to stay in bed – warding off an attack. Bobby has sore eyes, Dr. put "silver" in. Negadis returned reporting Gov. has flown to A.A. for his family & will get here in 15 days. Rained!

January 19 – Timcut (baptism) very "slim," few A's here. Rained!

January 20 – My lover doesn't feel very well – sore side. Goffa mail last night. Forsberg heir [baby] due in June.

January 25 – Negedras Tesima came tonight reporting that "I's" will "reach" tomorrow. May they! Dr. and Mrs. O. tried to clear up the matter concerning Lois & Dr.

January 26 – 3 cars & 3 trucks came into Soddu, at 10 a.m., stayed ½ hr. & returned to Setair'àh, leaving word the army etc. will come in the a.m. Oh may they!

January 27 – They did! At 10 a.m. – 4,000 native troops, Somalies, Eritrians, Tiger Clans, etc., tanks, trucks, cannon (field guns), white troops 1000, 5000 in all. We spoke with several who understood English. Mr. P. & "Pop"a. rode to town in a truck. Allen and Norm took animals & went to meet them. Many are camped below us – others at Johanns' late. Junior has a very bad eye. What an exciting day. Relief is great and appreciated. God is good.

January 28 – Many trucks passing. Fellows all are friendly. Somalies, etc. causing trouble to W's [Walamos]. Tesifa gone all a.m. hunting his horses – Tuncule washed(!) all to be done again tomorrow. He bought 1 T's tea!! from an Som. At 3 p.m. Hot dog – tea & four sandwiches. Raining.

January 29 – Fri. Trucks were supposed to leave for A.A. & Sidamo today – one fellow took our post – he gave Mr. A. & Alen each a chocolate bar which they kindly brot home & divided.

January 30 – [Hal's and Junior's birthday.] Had biscuits & jam for breakfast. Had sardine sandwiches and gifts at a late lunch at 3:30 – a gift from the Capt. Had Ray, John T. & Andersons for late supper. Played dominoes until 9:30. We had cochee-cochee for dinner with lemon fluff pie and mints!! Mrs. O. made the cake and jello!! Thank the Lord for the sugar. Hal got it from the Italians who would take no pay for it. Junior's left eye is so sore.

January 31 – Sunday – Had S.S. with our kiddies. Peg & Henry – my lover went to the camp with Mr. A. for stamps. Ray & O's went there for tea this p.m. at 4.

February 5 – We thot, a year ago, we would surely be enjoying this day at M. B. I. "As for God, His way is perfect!"

Junior's eye is well, thank God. My lover doesn't feel quite well, neither does Bobby. I hope his trouble isn't ears, since the rains continue.

February 7 – My lover spoke in evening – "Clouds." The first joint service since Miriam's illness in Nov. A good spirit – everyone present but Floss and Roberts.

February 8 – All men of station except John took our guns & ammunition for registration. Further request for planes for us. Capt. suggested Hal's going by plane & kiddies and I by truck, which Hal doesn't want if avoidable.

Mabel and Harold wearing Amhara, Ethiopia clothing, 1937

February 9 –Stayed in bed – resting. 5 Jimma carriers arrived, bringing sugar & flour. 2 did not come who have oil & flour. Played dominoes at O's in eve a short time. My lover beat in 2 games.

February 11 – Ray & "Pop" A got a little sugar & tea, which they shared, at camp.

February 11 – Still much rain – 2 wks now. Natives are plowing, etc.

February 12 – Made 2 cups strawberry preserves (Jimma sugar came recently, also flour) & had it for breakfast with hot biscuits. So good!

February 13 – My lover, Miriam, & Alen went to town in p.m. (The 3 boys & I had a long rest, baths etc. Hal dismissed Cassa & took on Tesfa's brother.) Bought 2 leopard skins (– 932 lire – $45 & $32 American) & Miriam's shoes ($8 M.T's) & 4 egg cups. No planes since 2 last Mon., when Hal went to the [Italians'] camp & rec'd promise of our request for plane to be answered by Fri. or Sat. from superior officer in Sidamo. Also said mail would come from A.A. by Sat. None came.

February 14 – Stayed in bed due to severe heart pain yesterday. Junior & I made hearts for table favors. Mr. O & 2 others went to I's to see what could be done for Wal & Enid who started here but had to stop 1 hr. from station. Clear weather today as was Fri. & Sat.

February 22 – Flew in an Italian bomber to A.A. – Trimotered bomber 1¾ hrs. – all nauseated, but Paul. Royal reception – living at M. Berger's, meals at Cains who are lovely.

February 27 – Sheila Engerts birthday party – Lewis, Shanks, M. P. & I attending. Had a surprise cake for me & another for Mrs. Bergman. Prayer Day, sweet time.

February 28 – Another cake (my 3rd) in eve. at Cains. Lunch at hdqtrs with Duffs, Cremers & Hal & I as guests, with tea & birthday cake for me in p.m. Gulalie folk over, for the latter.

March 1 – Spend a.m. shopping – G. Pogue, Hal, Mr. Duff & I.

March 2 – Spent day at Furi. Mr. Glover was taken to Gulalie – pneumonia. Hal took Junior, too, as he complained of ears. Had a sweet time with Mrs. Lewis.

March 3 – Intermission prayer meeting at Cains. Good spirits. My lover spoke. Mr. Duff returned without visa, so perhaps will not get away Fri., tho a cable left yesterday for New York stating that.

March 7 – Spent a.m. in bed as did Junior. My darling was asked to speak at a 4 P.M. on our experiences down country.

March 8 – Rec'd a letter today from Aunt Clara telling of Pete's death 1 yr. ago today. Wrote to Sarah & Roy, home (addressed to Rachel) Peters (St. Louis) Lambies, Tea at hdqtrs – Simpsons 2nd wddg. anniv. Dinner at 6 with Duffs.

March 10 – I went to the intermission prayer mtg. at the Barton's – good mtg. My lover was too tired to go. Cowers & Miss Bray came by plane this p.m.

March 11 – Final preparations – to bed at 11:15. (later – very little sleep as we were awake at four a.m. & up a bit later.)

March 12 – Went to station & came home again! Many of the dear ones here to bid us farewell, others prepared nice things, notes, etc. for us. My lover wasn't well so "all things," nevertheless. Many left, today.

March 13 – My lover is still in bed. I've spent most all of yesterday & today there, too. "B.C.M.S." [But Christ My Savior] boys all gone!

March 14 – Bobby has vomited about a dozen times. Nothing stays in his stomach. Junior has a very bad cold & cough. Paul's cold is improving. My lover is taking treatments from Mr. Shank. He is still in bed but got up to take the eve. service which proved to be a blessing.

March 15 – My lover is still in bed. Dysentery causes him, Bobby & I trouble – all getting same time castor oil, chlorodyne, soda, strict diet, etc. Bobby's milk was retained today – also a tiny bit of toast. Rohrbaughs left by plane this a.m. Immanuel gave a wonderful testimony: "only shortens our long journey, etc."

March 16 – My darling spoke at a meeting for all at Cains' tonight, continuing at their request last Sun. night's message.

March 17 – My lover gave another precious talk on the Tabernacle furniture as typing the Believer's walk, his third & last at tomorrow night, will have to pack for our leaving on Fri. D.V.

March 18 – My darling went to town to make (train) reservations.

March 19 – Left A.A. on a.m. train. Had much trouble getting seats & room for our feet, due to Greeks who'd taken every inch of room, reserved & otherwise. A very tiresome day & night.

March 20 – Arrived in Djibouti. Salle met us. Staying at Continental Hotel.

March 21 – Took the "Palestina" at 5 p.m. for Port Said. – a clean Italian boat with good meals – ice cream! Junior's & Bobby's colds are ugly. I'm taking it, too, I fear.

March 26 – Reached Port Suez – bought beads for Miriam & me.

March 27 – Arrived in Port Said – left for Cairo by car in p.m. viewing lovely Egypt en route – a 4 hr. drive.

March 28 – Visited temple & pyramids, sphinx & excavation scenes in a.m. – in p.m. – the museum & bazaar, attending Easter evening service at American Mission.

March 29 – Visited the zoo in a.m. – [King's] tombs, mosques & citadel in p.m. – bazaar early in eve. Had eve. parlor mtg. at American Mission.

March 30 – Visited the tombs of the kings (Memphis – at Sucarrah) in a.m. In p.m. tried to visit Mohammedan school & did visit the American Univ. of Cairo & rode around the city.

March 31 – Left Cairo by car about 8:30. Stopped in Zag Aziz from 10:30 till 1:30 with Misses Tait & Work. Had a sweet time of fellowship with them. Reached Cairo, had trouble with "Mr. Mick," who "went to the ship." We changed hotels & discharged him. My lover & I took a little stroll in the eve'g. buying his "mixed" suit. Late to bed & <u>tired</u>. Many Italian girls in hotel who came from Cairo to greet new ruler enroute to Ethiopia.

April 1 – In a.m., my lover looked after our visa, etc. for Palestine – made contract with our Cairo driver for him to take us to Palestine & return next Mon. Left Port Said at 3:30 p.m. – had supper in Port Suez. Traveled all night & got to the "Frontier" at cock-crow. Bobby's cold seems a little better. Paul is getting it. Passed 21 boats along the canal in p.m.

April 2 – Arrived in Jerusalem at noon – so tired after traveling all night from Port Said. The driver had no passport so had some trouble, which cleared up here. Staying at the "Shemariah Rest Home." Miriam breathes with difficulty. I wonder if it is only a cold & hate to leave her. Car has a broken spring so we are resting this p.m. a bit. We went to Gordon's Calvary, Garden of Gethsemane, saw the place of the skull, Jerusalem's 3 city walls, with various gates (sheep gate, Damascus gate, etc.)

April 3 – In a.m. in Jer. went to Bethlehem, Jer. Temple, saw Absolom's, etc. etc. tombs & Rachel's on road to Beth., saw many Jerusalem sights, Judas' garden, wells, etc. In p.m. went to Jericho, Dead Sea & Jordan River. What sacred places! What a privilege. God is <u>so</u> good to us!

April 4 – Bobby had to have an enema so Jr., he & I staid home while Hal, M. & P. went to the Church of the Holy Sepulcher, etc., returning at 11. Then Hal & I went to Alliance Church (Mr. Ralph Freid) – heard Dr. Cooper of Nashville on 1 Peter 1:3-5 – beautiful message – so precious to me. In p.m. went to John the Bapts. birthplace & village, so "locust trees," Zion, etc., Got photos, home for supper – wrote to Horns & packed.

April 5 – Up at 5 a.m., left at 6:45 (Jerusalem) to return to Port Said. 3 kiddies nearly sick with colds. God is able. Had lunch & supper enroute, including Jerusalem & Beersheba oranges. Had to make some stops due to Abdul's troubles. Arrived, finally at 8:30 in Port Said, tired, but thankful for all of God's journeying mercies. What a road! Flowers in the desert to brighten our trip – God's sweet care! P. & M. slept lots in a.m.

April 6 – A day of sleep – to become more fit for leaving the land. Our ship, due yesterday, is reported to be "in" tomorrow. Settled peacefully praise God, with Abdul, our Egyptian driver. Mr. Mick called today. Daddy & Paul took a walk on the sea shore, bringing back shells.

April 7 – I bought dress buttons & my hat. Had a restful day – finally getting over our return trip from Palestine. Miriam's cough is so severe, while Junior & Bobby have very sore ears still. We're using syringe, peroxide, salt water, etc. etc. Miriam & Daddy took a walk along the seashore. I laundered several things today. They dried rapidly. Good food here, too, at this "Hotel do la Poste."

April 8 – Left Port Said last night at midnight, getting another cabin overnight as the missionary (W. S. Presb.) from India & family who have my cabin are embarking at a.m. I changed cabins at breakfast time – the 3rd door from Paul & my lover. All Britians aboard, but us. Many children. Wonderful service! Meals grand & frequent – 6:30 tea; 9 a.m. break; 11 brief tea; 1, lunch; 4, tea; 7 dinner; 9:30 brunch!

April 9 – Did some laundering – got seasick in the hot, stuffy room.

April 10 – A rocky sea, so I'm seasick!!

April 11 – A good Sunday. My darling took "Church of England" service in a.m. & a non-sectarian one ("Modern Miracles in Modern Ethiopia") in eve. Wrote a letter or 2 today.

April 12 – Quiet day – wrote 6 or 7 letters, washed, ironed & mended & to bed early.

April 13 – (I was sick sick!! ugh! Jr. & Hal have bad headaches.) All told, 23 letters were mailed aboard the ship today, which were written since leaving Port Said last Wed. night. Had a "ship-wreck" party at dinner – paper hats, parasols, balloons, costumes, etc.

April 14 – Arrived in Marseilles, France about 1 p.m. or so. Went ashore to "sight-see," 2 hrs. Good trip. Read until 10 P.M. I'm taking more cold, I fear. 26 passengers went overland – 10 flying!

April 15 – Still in Marseilles. Cold, strong breeze, but sunny. Caught up my diary, did washing in a.m. Hal, M., P., & Charles Wallace went ashore. Put heavy undies on the kiddies & wish I had some!

April 24 – Packed in a.m., – going up the Thames today. Very cold night (last) p.m. & so was this a.m. Sun in p.m.

April 25 – Tied up in the Estuary (of Thames) over night. Mr. Abal (Allison's man) met us in Tilbury & took us to London where Eric H. met us & took us to Miss Gety's (10 Finchlin Road) at 2 p.m. In eve. Hal, Mr. & Mrs. Carnelly heard G. Campbell Morgan.

April 26 – Washed clothes, unpacked etc. Hal went to office in a.m, getting back [in evening].

April 27 – Blessed privilege – attended annual C.I.M. meeting this aft. – hearing Miss Francesca French – "Here's the Gospel Back Again."

May 2 – Attended "Portman Square – St. Paul." Collin Kerr in a.m. In eve. my lover spoke at a branch of the London City Mission, at Mr. Morgan's (John Trevin's friend) request. I staid at home.

May 3 – See Gal. 6:9. ["We shall reap, if we faint not."] Attended B.C.M.S. mtg. in eve. Shopped in a.m. – disappointing Syvilla Horn because it was impossible to accept their kind p.m. & supper invitation.

May 4 – Had a letter from Zan's Mrs. Allen. My darling met her son at the [Missionary] Training Colony this afternoon.

May 5 – Attended British & Foreign Bible Soc'y annual meeting – shopped – went to the office. Home at 5:45. In eve. my lover spoke in devotions at "House of Rest."

May 6 – Spent a.m. with work at home. Went down to the city at 2 p.m. – shopping, getting my lover's shoes & mine repaired etc. Visited in office with Mrs. Allen. Had tea with Mr. & Mrs. Horn, Mr. Ball, Miss Bayrum, my darling & I going to Caxton Hall for 7 p.m. service in which Mr. Hodgson (Tuarego) & Hal were the speakers from the fields. Home tired at 10:30 p.m.

May 7 – [London Eng. still.] Washed, packed & ironed all day. My lover had evening devotions here, he's been busy all day downtown & at office all day, Miriam & Paul going with him. Had cable from N.Y., okaying our funds plan.

May 8 – Left England, via "Manhattan" which was late, due to fog. Pleasant p.m. Lots of vibration, good cabins & food. Very little deck space, horrid lounge & nearly all foreigners in our class (3rd), but we'll manage the wk. okay with Xt [Christ] & for Him.

May 9 – Bad sea – many passengers seasick & we are not exceptions. "Mass" on board this a.m. We worshipped in our cabins.

May 10 – Rough sea all night, but improved by noon. Junior & I continue sick as well as Daddy so staid in bed until a.m. was well gone.

May 11 – Cold and foggy. Am reading (profitably) "Ambassadors for Xt"! My lover's glasses (bow) broke. "All things" & we're practically home so it will be alright.

May 12 – Warmer & foggy – some sun. Sat on deck quite a lot today. Dinner party tonight, balloons, "crackers," decorations 'n turkey. Kiddies were very much pleased.

May 13 – A beautiful, sunny, fairly warm day spent mostly on deck trying to "bake" out our colds. Wrote to Katherine, Sarah & Roy W. & Mrs. Christie.

May 14 – Foggy nearly all day. Packed. Have slowed down as we cannot dock before 9 a.m. tomorrow & are now nearly there. Breakfast is to be at 6:30 in the a.m. (Previously at 8:15.)

May 15 – New York City. Docked at 9:00 a.m. Met by Mrs. Trout, Lambie, Beeby, Adele & Gus, Mildred, P. B. & Mr. Bracham.

May 16 – Attended the Calvary Bapt. for S.S. & a.m. worship. Heard Dr. Rogers at 1st Bapt. in evening. Mildred & P. B. & Hal & I. Mr. P. spoke in S.S. at Gus & Adele's church. Dick Camp & family called in aft.

May 17 – Shopped in a.m. – got hat & 3 dresses – sox etc. My lover went to New York too, with others. Miss Hart & Mrs. Lambie & taking me – Jim L. chauffering. Mrs. Gran had luncheon – sightseeing – Dr. Vaughen attended Mr. Beacham's lecture in eve. – Tom Clark & wife came over.

May 18 – Hal went to Dr. Vaughen's for exam. Shopping, packing. Met Drs. B. & L. at dock – left for Allentown. Grand reception. Mtg in eveg at Peg & Miller Philip's parents' home. We stayed over night.

May 19 – Left for Newark, Ohio – at Aunt Minnie's, getting there just before dusk. So good to see everyone. To bed about 10:00 or so. All the family & relations there for dinner & the evening.

May 20 – Shopped (Aunt Minnie did.) Visited at Katherine's, back to Aunt M's for lunch – off for Paxton about 1 p.m., I think – getting there after sundown. Had informal reception at church. Mildred, P. B. & Mrs. B. at Arnolds'. M., P., & Jr. at Watts with Bobby. Hal & I at John Givens for the night.

May 21 – Left Paxton Ill. About 9:30 or so, after being down at Consumer's Store visiting, calling on Mrs. Gourley. Had lunch at Bieby's, supper at Burchs. Wonderful eve'g mtg in LaSalle church – many mothers responded to the altar call. Late lunch at Burchs – to bed at 2 a.m.!!

May 22 – Left LaSalle Ill. after Dr. Herbold treated Daddy & Paul. Got to Waterloo, in eve. Had prayer after B. & Jr. retired, to ascertain God's will concerning M. & P's going back to LaSalle for school & treatment.

May 23 – Prepared Miriam's & Paul's belongings for their return to LaSalle with the Bieby's. They left at 4 o'clock or so. Hal & I spoke in eve. service [at Walnut Street Baptist Church, P. B. is pastor]. Had sweet fellowship with Mildred & P. B. after church – chicken 'n all, too.

May 24 – Prepared for Jr. & Bobby to stay here [with P. B. & Mildred] & for Hal & I to go to St. Louis tomorrow.

May 25 –Took Harold, Jr. & B. to Wagner's as Miss Jenson wasn't home – left for St. L. at 5:10 – P. B. taking us to train. Whitney's refused any pay. How good our Father is to us & His own.

May 26 – Wonderful p.m. [prayer meeting] in eve. – Memorial Church, St. Louis. Maude greeted us when we got home. Ethel [H's sister] met us at train today.

May 27 – Went to church sewing circle – spoke briefly at noon luncheon. Attended p.m., prayer mtg. – Had p.m. in Mrs. Kotsreams, & Mizpah S.S. mtg in eveg. Terribly full day – too much. Every one friendly. Terribly weary. So is my lover.

May 28 – In p.m. my lover & I shopped – baggage, white shoes, etc – Wagners for dinner in evening. Wrote letter in a.m.

May 29 – Maude & I shopped in "Delmar" in a.m. Bought white hat in p.m. At Wagner's – Happy time of fellowship – fine mother. Welchs' & Mrs. Hall's in eve.

May 30 – A memorable day for Memorial Ch.! My lover had the services. 7 went forward in eve'g. – blessed time! Full day – weary, but so happy in our Lord's working. (Susan & Wilfred Wagner, Virginia K., Mary Bromhall, 2 young men & 1 stranger, young woman, went forward.)

May 31 – Slept 2 hrs. at noon. Kock's took us sightseeing 2 hrs. Miss Parker called in p.m. Had dinner with MacLeans – home early.

June 1 – Spoke 3 times at St. Louis noon center – Shopped all p.m., had dinner at home. Miss Lois Page called this a.m.

June 2 – Went to Miss R. Parkers – rec'd garments. – got out our general letter at church, had wonderful prayer mtg. – Simpsons, Kokks & girls taking us to train, which left St. L. for Waterloo at 11:30 p.m.

June 3 – Our train from St. Louis arrived 45 min. late. Mr. Titcomb & P. B. & Betty Mae met us in p.m. Jr. & B. came back. Jr. calmly said, "Hello," kissed us & said, "I want to ride the bicycle" Attended Mr. Titcomb's service in eve'g. Maude left for Mpls. [Minneapolis] today. We decided to go up there later.

June 4 – Chenaults [P. B. & Mildred] left for Mpls. [Minneapolis]. So glad for them & us as it is <u>good</u> to stop going! Hal & I had 1st treatments from Dr. Gottshall. (uterus slightly misplaced)

June 5 – Mildred & P. B. got home for lunch. It's quite cool today. Bobby & Harold Jr. are thrilled with their cars, a gift from Mrs. Mamie Hall of St. Louis. Attended banquet at church – good after mtg.

June 6 – I stayed home until 4:30 when the kiddies and I went with Mil & Carl to take gas to the gospel car. My lover & I attended Mr. Titcomb's last service here.

June 7 – In a.m., my darling & I washed.

June 8 – Had our second treatments with Dr. Gottshall in p.m. Ironed in p.m. (Bought Bobby's bed $12.) Wrote to Mrs. Barch about our staying in LaSalle 2 weeks, D.V. [Lord willing].

June 9 – Cooked mein for lunch – so good. In eve, Edna & Bill Kuhnle called. – a sweet couple. Had good letters from Miriam & Paul.

June 10 – Shopped & had my teeth examined. My lover doing the same in a.m. Had lunch with Cedarholms & "Wes. Eagen" – delightful time – musical glasses, violins, ice cream, type writers, etc. Home in eve.

June 18 – Had exam at Mayo Clinic. Maude & Helen Von Horn bringing us down here from Mpls. where we'd stay overnite at Dan & Ray Bergsten's. Staying at the Carlton Hotel. Full day of clinic exams. Raining, washed my hair. Tried to call Chenaults unable to get them.

June 19 – Busy all a.m. (till 1 p.m.) in clinic. Had a quick lunch & returned by bus to St. Paul reaching Maude about 5 p.m. Several visitors in eve.

July 1 – Spent night with Dolly & H. Berglund. [in Chicago]. Back to M.B.I. [Moody Bible Institute] (with K. McFarland.) – Visited Redpath, Benson & Cory, Holyworth, Christenson, "Hostess" –) Hockman [Houghton, Pres. of MBI], Allison Holly, etc – lunched with Mildred Erickson – Dr. Houghton & Mr. Christie walking over with us – Left skins at taxidermist's, back to Ed's [Cording] for dinner. In eve, visited with Hockmans, Wuests. Full, good day.

July 12 – Washed at Katherine's before going out to live at the hut. Fell & hurt my finger. Had all meals here.

July 19 – Washed & ironed at Margaret's & John's. Called on Schleiffers, Aunt Minnie's

July 20 – Had a family picnic here [in Newark] – 37 attended. Afterward Bobby S. & Clyde came. To bed late.

July 21 – Attended the prayer meeting at 1st Baptist Church – Dr. Crandle's invitation. Took Mrs. Coyle, Aunt Clara & Katherine home – called at Ned's, but he was not home. Hazel L. stayed until midnight. Had a good talk.

July 22 – Sewed at Grandmother's in a.m. Aunt Clara came home with us. Mrs. Stephan, Mrs. Mureen & children called in p.m., Mrs. S. bringing 4 jars of preserves & cookies. Rachel [sister] & family came in evening – also Ned. Visited Alma at the sanitorium.

July 23 – Went home with Aunt M. & Uncle John for lunch, then uptown to buy supplies for camp. (Aunt M. giving me $15 for same.) Bought materials, took the bus to Aunt Clara's where she, Grandmother & I made 6 single sheets, 3 table cloths & a night gown. Came home about 5:30 with my lover who had kept the kiddies at home all day at the farm. Early to bed. Wonderful moon & walnuts falling.

July 24 – Stayed home (hut) all day which was restful. In p.m., had a good rest, then prepared supper & food for tomorrow. Aunt M. & Uncle John & Clyde brot supplies. Came about 8:30 to tell us good-bye – leaving for Mich. early in a.m. Gave kiddies $2 each. Miriam rec'd a lovely birthday box from Maude – 2 dresses & 4 books. Bobby had a purse.

August 1 – Spoke (Hal & I) at Hyde Park Bapt. Ch. in a.m. – Dr. Hooper also. Spoke in S.S., too. In eve, heard Dr. T. T. Shieds at church. Took a sight-seeing ride afterward. In aft. the Donner's & Trenin sisters called on us here in the home. Tired.

August 2 – This is "Civic Day" in Canada. We've decided to leave in the a.m. for Ferndale.

August 3 – Reached Ferndale just as the noon blessing was being sung at lunchtime. Ethel & Ruth Parker warmly greeted us – in fact, everyone did except the one who should have & who never did during our brief stay as time proved.

August 4 – Stayed over, hoping, futilely, to have a better talk with Dr. B. [Bingham].

August 5 – Left at just 8 a.m. Had poor roads (& car trouble) & had to stay in Perth overnite.

August 6 – Reached Sand Bay in forenoon. Had a lovely reunion with Zan, Reg, & their relatives, having lunch & supper at Zan's. Went bathing [swim]!!

August 7 – This is an ideal spot for rest & relaxation.

August 8 – Hal, Ettie & I went to church in Shawville. The children attended a nearby S.S. Had the eve. service on the river-front. Mr. Fokes speaking.

August 13 – Reg & Hal accompanied Zan's father to Pembroke since he had to return due to the death of Jim Scarf's father. In p.m. I went fishing with Florence & Wallace. Caught nothing. Had supper there. Reg & Hal got home.

August 14 – Went boat riding in a.m. with Reg & Zan. In p.m., my lover went fishing & all the fishermen came here for supper. Reg & Wallace were called away.

August 15 – In a.m. I had Zan's kiddies & ours while she & Reg, Lyla, Wallace & Florence went to hear Hal at the Shawville church. In p.m. Reg, Ettie, Mrs. Newlan, Hal & I went to another place nearby, where my lover spoke – Reg presiding. In eve, Wallace spoke at the riverside here. Afterward Zan, Reg, Hal & I talked together & had prayer. Getting to bed at 11 p.m.

August 16 – This p.m. Reg & my darling left for Pembroke to be joined by Mr. Ward on a two day trip thru the Algonquin Forest.

August 17 – Zan slept with me last night as her lover & mine are in Pembroke. Lyla washed. I wrote MacLennon's in afternoon. Have headache today. Cloudy.

Chapter 7

All Things for the Gospel's Sake

The entry on August 17, 1937, was the final entry that Mabel Street made in her Five-Year Diary. Her effort emphasized her experiences in Ethiopia, where God had led them to minister. God was always with them through trials and joys. Their desire was to live in obedience to the Lord and to bring glory to Him. They encountered hardships as they served those in need.

To live in primitive, remote, and physically challenging areas of interior Ethiopia required sacrifice. They lived in mud brick, thatched roof homes with dirt floors and no modern conveniences of electricity, running water or indoor plumbing. This lifestyle was a stark contrast from their former business years of affluence and comfort.

Their strong faith and their belief that God had called them to reach out with His love to nationals, who were mostly pagan, was compelling. The family often faced severe health issues that hampered their efforts.

The Streets were aware of the need to study the language, customs and traditions of the natives to succeed in ministry. Much time and effort was devoted toward this goal. Often the natives did not know how to read or write. Culturally, they practiced customs that were passed on from generation to generation by word of mouth and by example. Most of these natives practiced paganism and were unaware of the Christian message and the new life possible as believers.

Early efforts of Harold and Mabel and other missionaries focused on reducing the language to writing, an arduous and slow process. Next was to teach the nationals to read and comprehend for those involved. The missionaries also translated from the Bible the Book of Mark for the natives' use.

Additional efforts were devoted to provide medical and agricultural assistance. Sometimes they encountered resistance, but through examples of positive changes, over time, these modifications were embraced.

Harold and Mabel ministered in very difficult situations with extreme challenges, but they also experienced opportunities of joy. They served the Lord out of love for Him. God blessed their efforts and was glorified.

Mabel did not record in her Diary an experience that is noteworthy. It was related to Mabel by Christian believers who witnessed the experience. Hostile natives had previously taken Harold, a prisoner in chains, to their village. Mabel and the "kiddies" had gone to sleep in their home. While they were sleeping, hostile natives carrying lighted (burning) torches approached the house to burn it down. As they neared the house, they looked up on the thatch roof to see an amazing sight. Standing on the roof were men (guardian angels) dressed in white protecting the Streets. The hostile natives fled with fright and those inside the house had their lives spared. The reporting believers called this incident a miracle as the family was spared from harm. They all marveled and rejoiced at the power and love of God.

As the date and time of this event was later shared with those from one of the supporting churches in Illinois, it was noted that at that specific time the church members were earnestly and specifically praying for the safety and care of the Streets. What an example of God's specific answer to the prayers of His people.

When God called the Streets into His service, He promised in His Word never to leave or forsake them. Their lives were spared so that they might continue to reach out with His love to others in need.

Chapter 8

The Mission Continues

The missionaries were forced to leave Ethiopia because the Italians, under the leadership of Mussolini, conquered their country. In 1936, the Italians captured Addis Ababa, the capital. Emperor Haile Selassie fled to England. In 1941, Ethiopian guerillas, aided by British forces, freed the nation and Haile Selassie returned as Emperor. In 1945 Ethiopia joined the United Nations.

When missionaries began leaving the country in 1936, many were disappointed and thought that the small band of believers there would face pressures that would cause them to forsake their belief. But God!

"Our Daily Bread" ("Much More Than Survival" by C. P. Hia, January 13, 2014) states, In April 1937, "Mussolini's invading armies forced all the missionaries serving in the Walamo region to flee Ethiopia. They left behind just 48 Christian converts, who had little more than the gospel of Mark to feed their growth. Few even knew how to read. But when the missionaries returned 4 years later, the church had not just survived; it numbered 10,000!"

Oh, what a God! Some plant, some water, but God gives the increase.

When the Streets returned to New York, they were greeted at the ship by P. B. and Mildred Chanault, good friends and supporters. P. B. was a classmate of Harold at Moody in the Pastor's Course. He was also the pastor of the Walnut Street Baptist Church in Waterloo, Iowa, one of the supporting churches of the Streets.

Since the family had health issues that began in Ethiopia and prohibited them from returning to Africa, Harold continued his ministry as a Deputation Secretary for the Sudan Interior Mission. In this capacity, he held meetings in various churches to help raise funds and support for other missionaries going to the mission field. The mission leaders determined that the Streets should move to Wheaton, in the Chicago area as their base of operations.

In 1937 when the family moved to Wheaton, the public schools tested Miriam and Paul and found them to be functioning below normal. Miriam, an eleven-year-old, performed at a third-grade level. Paul, a ten-year-old, was placed in first grade. These early years in public school were a difficult time for Miriam and Paul. The Streets hired a teacher, Jean Reynolds, to live with them and to tutor Paul and Miriam.

The family moved in 1938 to Waterloo, Iowa, for the next few school years, where Harold continued as Deputation Secretary for Sudan Interior Mission. Miriam and Paul made progress in school with the help of the classroom teachers and tutorial help but remained behind in classroom performance for their age.

In addition to his work for SIM, Harold did some teaching at a Bible college started by the staff at Walnut Street Baptist Church. Work continued for SIM in Iowa until 1941 when the family moved to Minneapolis, Minnesota. Miriam ultimately functioned at grade level for her age. The three other children graduated from high school in Minneapolis. When Paul graduated from high school, he was one year older than his classmates. His size and skill enabled him to excel as a lineman on the varsity football team.

Junior did well in school, played three years on the varsity tennis team, was a Student Council member and sometimes served as the master of ceremonies at school assemblies.

Bobby went to Minnehaha Academy, receiving personalized assistance in a smaller school, and graduated in 1953.

With Harold's heavy schedule of meetings, often the time spent with the family was limited. One year, Harold was able to be at home only fourteen days. When asked about this sacrifice, he responded that even though he missed the family, he knew that God had called him into ministry as a priority and that God would bless and keep his family from harm.

Another time Harold was asked if he ever regretted giving up his comfortable life at Heinz for a life of struggle, hardship, and sacrifice in Ethiopia. His response was emphatic: "Not for a minute. The rewards for doing the Lord's work far outweigh any value that the world provides. I'm so grateful for the opportunity to love and serve my Lord and to bring glory to His Name!"

Street Family at Harold and Mabel's 25th wedding anniversary, September 27, 1949 at their Minneapolis, MN, home

The Mission Continues • 135

In 1955 Ken Taylor, author of the "Living Bible" and founder of Tyndale Publishers, along with Pete Gunther, a co-worker at Moody Bible Institute, established Evangelical Literature Overseas. It was an organization that worked with 123 worldwide mission boards and organizations to identify worthy literature projects that needed funding for publication. Ken Taylor and Pete Gunther, along with their Board of Directors, asked Harold to join them in 1955 as Executive Secretary of Evangelical Literature Overseas. Harold and Mabel prayed about this challenging opportunity and sought to know God's will for them. They felt led by God to respond affirmatively, and joined E. L. O., moving back to Wheaton, Illinois, to head up this work.

Their responsibility required frequent international travel to provide counsel, raise support for the projects, and help with the publication of materials. The Street children were in college or military service, so Mabel was free to travel with Harold. The Lord blessed the ministry with E. L. O. Again they were able to thank the Lord for His calling and His enabling in their service for Him.

Harold at a world map as Executive Secretary of Evangelical Literature Overseas, 1962

Harold also wrote two books, which Moody Press in Chicago published. *God's Home in the Believer* for mature Christians, and a children's book, *Billy Catches a Vision*.

In 1963, Harold and Mabel left Evangelical Literature Overseas to work for the Billy Graham Evangelistic Association in Honolulu, Hawaii. Harold and Mabel became managers of the KAIM Christian Bookstore and assisted with the KAIM Christian radio station there. Harold taught at the International Bible College in Honolulu. They also taught Bible classes in the local churches of Honolulu. To live in an area with such beauty and with such moderate climate was a blessing after being in harsher climates. Frequently, they returned to the mainland to attend meetings of Christian Booksellers and other Christian conferences. They also enjoyed visiting family and friends on the mainland.

Harold and Mabel in front of KAIM Bookstore, Honolulu, Hawaii, 1969

The Mission Continues • 137

On August 15, 1969, Harold preached in a church in Honolulu and was on the way to speak in another when he was in an auto accident that took his life. At his memorial service it was said, "He had an unusual ability to make Bible truths understandable and real." He often would say, "Head's up, knees down." He lived for 70 years, suffered two heart attacks and had several other health issues attributed to his time spent in Ethiopia, but God had called him into ministry, and he obeyed God's calling. Harold showed the Lord's blessing through love in a life dedicated to Christ and His glory.

After Harold's call to be with his Lord, Mabel returned to Wheaton to be near her children and grandchildren and to speak in various churches. She dedicated her life to show God's love to those in need. After a battle with pancreatic cancer, the Lord called her home in 1988 to be with Him.

Harold and Mabel loved the Lord, loved each other and loved their children. Each child had health issues in Ethiopia, which produced some weaknesses that impacted their later years. Early on, the children learned to trust God for His leading in their lives. God guided and protected them over the years.

God blessed all four Street children and their families as they, too, love and serve the Lord.

When God called Harold and Mabel into service for Him, little did they know what would result. They responded to His call with love, and God blessed their ministry over the years with many, many changed lives. Mabel and Harold loved God first. They also deeply loved each other, and they loved their children. God greatly blessed their lives of sacrifice and service. They have left an amazing heritage – a godly legacy. In the extended family are the following:

- 17 graduates of Moody Bible Institute
- 20 graduates of Wheaton College (most with graduate degrees)
- 8 have doctorates, and one is almost finished
- 3 college or seminary professors

- 1 surgeon
- 1 dentist
- 1 lawyer
- 1 city administrator
- Pastors, teachers, school administrators, business people, nurses, engineers, missionaries
- All are believers! Praise God!

Their daughter, Miriam, became a reading specialist, and she and her husband, Dr. Mel Holsteen (seated on the far left), in Ethiopia under the Sudan Inland Mission. Miriam and Mel's daughter, Carole, a linguist, and her husband, Dr. Gord Sawatzky, devoted their lives in service to many people groups in Nigeria, Kenya, and South Sudan with the Africa Inland Mission.

Harold and Mabel led by example. Their love for God was modeled for the family and others to observe. They often struggled and lived sacrificially in response to serve the God they loved in obedience. Although they encountered severe challenges, they also witnessed God's blessings and experienced the joy of the Lord as He rewarded their efforts for eternity.

Chapter 9

Reflecting on God's Blessings

That None Should Perish, Ethiopia 1933-1937 is a glimpse into the daily lives of Mabel and Harold Street while on the foreign mission field in Ethiopia and in the U.S. with the Sudan Interior Mission. After their return from Ethiopia, Harold served as Executive Secretary for Evangelical Literature Overseas and finally as managers of the KAIM Bookstore in Honolulu, Hawaii. God blessed each of these efforts.

First, Mabel and Harold loved the Lord and were obedient to His calling on their lives. This was a wonderful relationship! As they studied God's Word, their faith and service opportunities increased. God's word of "Go into all the world and preach the Gospel, and lo, I am with you always" was evident in their love relationship with their Lord. They constantly proved God's love for them, and they expressed their love for Him by obeying Him in their lifelong journey.

> Sometimes we learn that hardships
> Were blessings in disguise,
> That earnest work and faith in God
> Were proven to be wise.
>
> —Hermann Hesse

Secondly, Harold and Mabel loved each other. They constantly expressed their love for each other by word and deed. Each one tenderly cared for and served the other as a priority in their love relationship. Those who knew them often marveled at their love for the Lord and their sacrificial love for each other.

Thirdly, the love of God working through Mabel and Harold as they expressed their love for their "kiddies." Their home was Christ-centered, consistently encouraging deep love and respect for one another. Each day, Harold and Mabel led the family in the study of God's Word and in prayer. Even though the family faced many trials, the environment of love resulted in each child making a personal commitment to accept Christ as Savior at an early age. Harold and Mabel encouraged their children to grow in their Christian journey.

How God blessed these lives devoted to love and serve their heavenly Father! The Streets' lives of sacrifice and hardship were often difficult, but they felt compelled to serve their God. He is God, who loves the world including the United States and Ethiopia, Africa. Eternity will reveal the full impact of lives expended in service for the glory of God.

That None Should Perish, Ethiopia 1933-1937 was written to share the journey of Mabel and Harold and the "kiddies." May this story with its challenges and victories inspire your life.

Chapter 10

Childhood Memories of Hal and Paul

HAL

Family members have related the following incidents that occurred in my early years.

As a toddler in Ethiopia, I enjoyed being outside when the weather was nice. As a one-year-old and unsteady in walking, I went out into the yard where there were several young chickens. As I leaned over to try and pick up one of the chickens, I lost my balance and sat down on another chicken, upsetting me and killing the chicken.

In remote Ethiopia, without indoor plumbing, it was necessary to use an outhouse. Mother was taking me to use the outhouse. As she opened the door to the outhouse, we were startled to see a poisonous snake inside. She quickly pushed the door shut and we made a quick exit, thanking the Lord for His protection.

As a three-year-old, I was outside and encountered a colony of Army ants crossing the area. These large black ants are very aggressive, and my curiosity was my downfall. The ants crawled over my body, biting as they went. I screamed with pain and my parents came running out to help. They pulled me away, brushed off the ants, and pulled off my clothes. Dad quickly got some kerosene and a rag to help extricate the biting ants.

Bathing with hot soapy water helped to remove the kerosene. Medicine and lotion were applied to the bites and I had no further allergic reaction. Praise was offered to God for His care and healing.

The family was back in Soddo in August/September of 1936 when I was 4 years old. Johannes, an Ethiopian boy of 13 and a helper around the house and yard, was also at times a playmate for Miriam and Paul. At this time, the family dog, Sue, had contracted rabies, unbeknownst to the family. Sue bit Johannes, Miriam, Paul, and me. Each of us was treated with nitric acid on the bites, and Sue was shot. Over a two- or three-week period, Johannes got sick with considerable pain over time. Miriam, Paul, and I did not show any symptoms of illness. The doctor stated that Johannes' illness was the result of Sue's bite. Mother wrote in her diary, "Praise God the kiddies didn't develop anything after [Sue's] bites." My sister, brother, and I were spared adverse effects of Sue's bites. I still have scars on my wrist from the bites. I warn people that if they see me start to foam at the mouth, to watch out!

PAUL

In September 1936, Sue, our family dog, got out of our fenced yard and was bitten by a rabid dog. After an incubation period, she developed rabies.

Miriam, Paul, Junior, and Johannes, an Ethiopian helper and playmate, were playing in the yard when we were each bitten by Sue. Each wound was cauterized with nitric acid.

A few days after we were bitten, Johannes developed symptoms that were painful, followed by irrational behavior including violent mouth and throat spasms. He was confined to a room where the window and door were boarded up. A slot was kept in the door to pass food and water to Johannes. He would fall asleep on the floor, get up, and run from side to side of the room screaming until he would drop from exhaustion. He died at 4:00 p.m., September 30.

How the family thanked and praised the Lord for His protection from rabies for the other children—Miriam, Paul, and Junior.

Mother would normally spend time with each child at bedtime sharing a Bible story, a song, and would pray before saying good night.

The night of Johannes' death, I was hesitant to pray and was distressed. I expressed my fear of dying like Johannes and not knowing his future.

Mother lovingly and gently shared Christ's love for me and God's plan of salvation for those who trust in Him. Christ's death on the cross to pay for our sins and His resurrection over sin and death provides salvation for those who ask forgiveness and trust in Christ for salvation and eternal life.

I prayed for forgiveness of my sins and trusted Christ as my Savior that night. Immediately, I sensed peace and joy, and comfort as I became a child of God. The result was a peaceful night's sleep.

The family was grateful for my decision for Christ and God's protection from rabies.

Chapter 11

Surprise! Small World

In the fall of 2015, I went to eat dinner at the Home Plate Restaurant near Hot Springs Village, Arkansas. I sat in a booth near where patrons added their names to a list used to seat individuals when space was available. The tables were occupied when Lyle and Sharon Sands came to sign in. Recognizing them from Village Bible Church, I invited them to join me and avoid the wait to be seated. They came over and sat down, we placed our order for food and began our conversation.

We were slightly acquainted through church, but this gave us an opportunity to become better acquainted. It turned out that Sharon had also grown up in Minneapolis and attended high school there. She had gone to South High, and I attended West High. Small world.

I told them that I was writing a book based on a five-year diary that Mother had written while we were missionaries in Ethiopia. In addition, I shared the other ministries they had served with, concluding with the time they spent as managers of the KAIM Christian Bookstore in Honolulu, Hawaii for the Billy Graham Evangelistic Association.

Sharon exclaimed, "Hal Street! Honolulu, Hawaii! We knew him while Lyle was in the Navy, and we were stationed in Honolulu. We attended the same church as charter members of the International Baptist

Church in Honolulu. Jim Cook was pastor, and Hal Street often spoke or led Bible Studies." Sharon also worked in the KAIM Christian Bookstore as part of the Child Evangelism outreach.

This was astounding! After all these years from the mid-to-late 1960s until the fall of 2015, this "chance meeting" brought us together in a bond that was wonderful for us as members of the family of God. As we parted, we hugged, grateful for this special opportunity to recapture God's leading.

Shortly after our meeting, she contacted friends who had been stationed in the Navy in Honolulu at about the same time as the Sands. These friends had recently moved to Texas, and Sharon shared with them the conversation at the restaurant. The friends stated that they had a picture of Hal Street leaving the church after he had spoken there. They thought that his family would enjoy having the <u>last</u> picture of Hal Street and sent it to Sharon. Shortly after the picture was taken, Hal Street was on his way to speak in another church when he was in a fatal auto accident.

Years later, Hal was quoted in the E.L.O. Bulletin (Vol. 12, No.2), copyright 1969, written by James Johnson, Executive Secretary of Evangelical Literature Overseas:

> *I remember what he said when he took up his ministry in Hawaii—"Don't keep looking at your feet, you're bound to fall flat on your face. Keep your eyes on the horizon where the <u>Daystar</u> rises, from where the mountains meet the sky, from whence comes our help and where God will show you what's in store. God wants 'tall' men, and you don't grow much staring at the ground; it's when you stretch to see <u>Him</u> and <u>His</u> plan for you that you reach your full stature."*

Dr. James R. Cook was the senior pastor of the International Baptist Church in Honolulu where Hal and Mabel were members. Below is his letter he sent with a brief insight into their ministry in Hawaii.

Dear Hal:

I just want you to know how much we loved your folks and thankful to the Lord for all they did for the ministry there. This ministry became worldwide in its scope as hundreds of young people went all over the world and our country. The count when we had the 50th anniversary was stunning. During the first 16 and 1/2 years over 500 went into full-time service around the world. This fact came out during the Jubilee Celebration of the church when people from all over the world came to celebrate what the Lord had done. I want you to know that your dad and mom were part of that miracle. I will be forever grateful for their lives and for the contribution to the worldwide ministry for the Lord.

[Rev. and Mrs. Street were] in leadership and also [taught] Sunday school, in an adult class. We then started International College and Graduate School, where he taught a very special class on Ministry Options. During that time, the ministry grew in a tremendous way.

We ended up having five services every Sunday, three in the morning starting at 8:00 a.m. and two services in the evening. These services were all packed to capacity. Rev. and Mrs. Street were a great part of that ministry time, including being on KAIM radio five days a week.

One Sunday morning, as we were preparing for the second service, we heard an incredible crash on the street in front of the church and a very Special Servant of the Lord was called home to his reward. This was a tremendous shock to all the Christian Community of Hawaii and especially to us all. A tremendous void was left in all our hearts and the Christian ministry in the islands.

Thankful to the Lord,

Dr. James R. Cook

God, who had called the Streets into ministry many years earlier and had enabled them to have many years of faithful service, now called him "home" to glory for eternity.

Appendix A

People and Places in the Diary

Family:

Harold Street – Father: Lindley Street
    Mother: Ida Mae Street
    Sisters: Maude and Ethel

Mabel Street – Father: John Henry Ellis
    Mother: Kathryn Elizabeth
    Brothers: John, Roderic, Ned, Clyde
    Sisters: Rachel, Katherine
    Aunt: Minnie

Children – Miriam, Paul, Harold (Junior), John Robert (Bobbie)

Missionaries in Ethiopia

Dr. Rowland Bingham – Director Sudan Interior Mission

Dr. Thomas Lambie – Field Director

Mr. Ohman – Field Director

Mr. & Mrs. Anderson

Mrs. Bancroft

Dr. & Mrs. Borch-Jensen

Miss Bray, Nurse

Mr. Cain

Mr. & Mrs. Colson

Mr. & Mrs. Cowsers

Mr. & Mrs. Davidson

Don & Ruth Davies

Ray Davis

C. Duff

John & Peg Forsberg

Dr. Donald Hockman – Performed gall bladder surgery on Harold. Was killed while dismantling an Italian bomb.

Dr. & Mrs. Hooper

Mr. & Mrs. Horn

Mr. & Mrs. Jensen

Dr. & Mrs. Kirk

Dr. & Mrs. Lewis

Mr. Martin – language teacher

Dr. Orr – died of typhus

Mr. & Mrs. Parks

John & Peg Phillips

Dr. Pollock – eye specialist

Dr. Quitenham – from Sidamo

Dr. John & Peg Roberts – Treated and performed surgery on the Streets and others

Mr. & Mrs. Roke

Wyn Robertson

Mr. Russell

Dick & Audry Sanford

Mr. & Mrs. Smith

Mr. & Mrs. Southard – U.S. Ambassador

Mr. & Mrs. Walker

Mrs. Wilson

Supporters

LaSalle, IL – Baptist

Paxton, IL – Presbyterian

Waterloo, IA – Walnut Street Baptist Church

Pastor P. B. and Mildred Chanault

Many other individuals in the U.S.

Ethiopian Leaders

Haile Selassie – Emperor, fled country with Italian conquest
   Tribal Leaders:
    Dejazmatch Bunna
    Fitawrari Sailies – Gultitas (referenced in diary as "Feteraries")
    Fitawrari Danya

Local Ethiopians – mail carriers, helpers, cooks

Negadis – Native mail carriers. Used mules.

Bahone

Balacho

Bocca

Bocula

Buna

Cossah (Coso)

Digago

Dirsita

Giza

Gubamudeem (Gub)

Guburo

Gudana

Ibota

Iraba

Johannes – bitten by rabid dog, Sue, and died

Makonnen

Tabech

Tesima

Tiginia

Togalie

Tola

Locations

Addis Ababa – capital of Ethiopia

Akaki – Inter-mission center, one hour from Furi

Azoh – near Gamo

Baroda – near Soddo

Chincha – near Gamo

Dorsey – south of Soddo

Furi – mission station near Addis Ababa

Gamo – far south near border

Gulcho – near Soddo

Lamenda – near Addis

Ochola – near Gamo

Shammah – 1¾ hour north of Chincha

Soddo/Soddu (spellings interchangeable)

Wabarel – near Gamo

Celebrations

Timcot – January 25, Ethiopian festival

Ethiopia's Easter – April 8, end fast

Tribes – often at war with each other

Amharas

Dieta (Deta)

Dorays

Gulta

Sharahs

Shamas

Wobaras

Horses

Rhoada – brown

Pax – white – purchased with gift from Paxton, IL, supporting church

Dogs

Pru

Sue – contracted rabies and was shot

Native food

Watt

Ingeria

Appendix B

Quotes from Mabel's New Testament

Being ever-sensitive to the Spirit of God, Mabel noted inspirational verses and messages from many sources on the blank pages of her little New Testament, which had been a gift from her children in 1931. She continued saving notes for many years beyond her mission years in Ethiopia, and she carried her inscribed New Testament with her wherever she spoke. These handwritten notes reveal her love for the lost—that none should perish.

The restless millions wait the Light
Whose dawning maketh all things new.
Christ also waits, but men are slow and few.
Have we done all we could? Have I? Have you?

(*Sources*: Corrie ten Boom lecture–http://www.sermonindex.net/modules/newbb/viewtopic.php?topic_id=15978&forum=34
S. D. Gordon sermon–https://biblehub.com/library/gordon/quiet_talks_with_world_winners/christ_also_waits.htm)

"Missions represents not a human devise, but a Divine enterprise."

                                              (A. T. Pierson, 1837–1911)

"Christ alone can save this world
But Christ cannot save this world alone."

                                                        (A. T. Pierson)

"He Was Not Willing"

Perishing, perishing,
Hark how they call us!
Give us your Savior
O, tell us of Him.

We are so weary,
So heavily laden
And with long weeping
Our eyes have grown dim.

                                          (Lucy J. Meyer, 1849–1922)

"What a glorious work
Awaits _you_ in this land!"

                                                           (Unknown)

Psalm 135:14-18 – Idols of heathen will perish.
2 Peter 3:9 – The Lord is … not willing that any should perish, but that all should come to repentance.

Let compassion for sinners be found in me
China, India, Africa, o'er the sea,
Southlands, bound and not free
Islands, deep in the sea.
Let compassion for sinners be found in me.

(Unknown)

My album is a savage breast
Where darkness reigns
and tempests wrest.
Without one ray of light.
To write the name of Jesus there,
To point to mansions bright and fair,
To see the savage kneel in prayer,
Is my supreme delight.

(Robert Moffat, 1795–1883)

"This Bible is about
Ruin and Redemption."

(D. L. Moody, 1837–1899)

What are you doing for missions? 1 Cor. 15:34

Personal work plan:

Rom. 3:10, "None righteous ...
3:23, "All have sinned ...
6:23, "Wages," "gift of God is" ...
10:13, (9-13) "Whosoever shall call upon the name of the Lord shall be saved" (assurance)
John 5:24 "hath everlasting life" ...
1 Jn 5:10-12 "hath the Son hath life" ...

Fret not, He loves you. Jn. 13:1
Faint not, He holds you. Ps. 139:10
Fear not, He keeps Thee. Ps. 121:5

What place does practical training have in preparation for Christian service:

Being born again
Know how to win others to Christ—"by all means, save some."
What place do builders, gardeners, teachers, nurses, doctors, dentists? Broad training in every field vs. specialists.

Divine occupation
Divine ownership
Divine operation
1 Cor. 6:19 (20)

Your body is the temple of the Holy Spirit. Who is in you?
Obedience precedes blessing.

"No interest in missions betrays either a woeful ignorance or a willful disobedience."

(M. D. Babcock, 1858–1901)

Looking backward, we can say "Ebenezer" (1 Sam. 7:12) Hitherto hath the Lord helped us.
Looking forward, we can say "Jehovah-Jireh" (Gen. 22:14) The Lord will provide.
Looking upward, we can say "Jehovah-Shalom" The Lord send peace.
Looking onward, we can say "Jehovah-Shammah" (Ezek. 48:35) The Lord is there for the future.

God's will is the one fount of undefiled peace and joy. To do that will at any cost has become the passion of my life (entered May 1, 1932, the year they were called to be missionaries).

(Unknown)

It will not seem hard in heaven
To have followed the steps of our Guide. Acts 19:20

(Unknown)

Notes:

1. Recognize that you are not a Christian because you are good

2. Because you're doing the best you can

3. Because you are a church member

4. Confess that you are a guilty sinner in God's sight

5. That you are hopelessly lost and under condemnation without Jesus Christ as your personal Savior

6. Confess that you cannot save yourself

7. Believe the good news – He died for you and settled your sin debt on Calvary's Cross

8. Christ was raised from the dead and by the power of God is now able to save

9. Call upon the name of God in prayer and desire to be saved from your sins, for God has promised

10. Rely on God's promise, not your feelings, and declare you are saved by the blood of Jesus Christ, shed for the forgiveness of your sins and openly confess Him with your mouth as your Savior and Lord.

Salvation:

John 3:16 & 35; 5:24

Heb. 9:22

1 John 1:7 & 9; 5:12

How to become a Christian:

Rom. 3:12 & 23; 2 Tim. 3:5; Romans 3:19; Eph. 2:8; Luke 19:10; Rom. 5:8; Heb. 7:25; Rom. 10:13; Rom. 9-10.

Scriptures on indigenous church:

Acts 14:23 – Self-governing

1 Cor. 16: 1-2 – Self-supporting

1 Thess. 1:7-8 – Self-propagating

2 Cor. 6:14 – On probation

"Others"

Lord, help me live from day to day,
    In such a self-forgetful way,
That even when I need to pray,
    My prayer shall be for – Others.

Help me in all the work I do
    To ever be sincere and true,
And know that all I'd do for you,
    Must needs be done for – Others.

Let self be crucified and slain
    And buried deep: and all in vain,
May efforts be to rise again,
    Unless to live for – Others.

Others, Lord, yes – Others,
    Let this my motto be;
Help me to live for – Others,
    That I may live like Thee.

(Charles D. Meigs, public domain)

CPSIA information can be obtained
at www.ICGtesting.com
Printed in the USA
FFHW011907010319
50760176-56178FF